AT TIMES I SEE

HUUB OOSTERHUIS

At Times I See

Reflections, Prayers,
Poems, and Songs

TRANSLATED BY Redmond McGoldrick
ASSISTED BY Ger Groot
in collaboration with the author

A CROSSROAD BOOK
The Seabury Press · New York

The Seabury Press
815 Second Avenue
New York, N.Y. 10017

Original title: *Zien Soms Even*
Originally published in Dutch by Uitgeverij Ambo
© 1972 by Uitgeverij Ambo
English translation copyright © 1974 by The Seabury Press

Designed by Paula Wiener
Printed in the United States of America

Library of Congress Cataloging in Publication Data
Oosterhuis, Huub.
    At times I see.

    "A Crossroad book."
    Translation of Zien, some even.
    I. Title.
PT5881.25.08Z713   839.3'1'164   74-13002
ISBN 0-8164-1177-8

ACKNOWLEDGMENTS

I gratefully acknowledge the assistance (word by word) of Ger Groot, the patient and careful collaboration of the author, and the helpful suggestions made by many people. The occasional Notes, indicated * *or* ** , found on pp. 164–166 are mine.
Amsterdam
December 1973

Redmond McGoldrick
translator

Contents

THE SCRAP

He stood there in the shop. Clearance Sale. The rustle of wrapping paper and dollars at the head of the line. His turn.

"Two inches of God, please," he said.

"Can we make that four, sir? I have a scrap of goods here, just four by four. Then I won't have to cut any."

"Right. Just wrap it up, please."

He paid the usual price.

Outside again, he stepped cautiously over the slippery ripples of frozen snow, mumbling to himself, "What shall I do with this scrap? It's too small to sleep on, too soft to build a house on, too expensive to make clothes out of. But just for fun, I could easily send it to somebody to use as a Band-Aid. Or send it imprinted with a kiss, or with something written on it about someone I love, maybe."

Still mumbling, he took care not to slip on the ice. And he walked, year after year, took to the sky now and then, while his eyes asked the light, his feet asked the ground, and his hands asked each other, "What shall I do with this scrap?"

NAMED

Divided distraught without peace of mind
doomed to dispute and to fight with myself
like her who once wrote *I loathe that I live.**
And yet, in your hands and named after you.

❧ SEEING

this that
yes no
driving driven
cannot will not
yet must
live so,
everywhere nowhere
no one in sight.
Then you.
I hear your voice,
at times I see.

❧ PLACES ENOUGH

Places enough where one can hear God-talk, and occasions. There is an impressive vocabulary, often a rather imprecise jargon in which a "concept of God" comes wrapped up. No one perceives it clearly, no one possesses it, but it is there. And it plays its part among all peoples. Indeed it is subsidized, accorded shared-time, and inspires strong words about good and evil. The idea of God is poised unsteadily upon a pedestal of reasoning and dogma, as upon the point of a needle.

There doesn't happen to be a world without a concept or image of God. If there were, maybe it would be a relief. True, we might think about one and proclaim it. But in vain, for a concept of God simply *is*. Only one?

About the word *god*. Probably derived, say the scholars, from the original Indo-Germanic, the ancestral language of "our" inhabited world. To be precise, from the word *ghu-to, the called one (or thing),* from the same stem as an old Norse word meaning *to bark* and an ancient Indic word meaning *he calls to.* So much for *god*. From Iceland to India, from North Ireland to East Pakistan, reaching back at least 3,000 years: *he who is called?* or *he who calls?*

I notice people saying *God* with all kinds of inflections, in all kinds of situations. Often it is a handy word, a common place where people can find each other, where they can reveal to each other their noblest intentions and boldest dreams. God as a rallying point. God, a wink of recognition.

God, a wall of glass between people, a strange noise? A word which separates people from each other?

Nowadays most people are no longer afraid of God. Formerly they were. He used to come into their yards, mean and slobbering, like a dog, grimly jealous, unpredictable, the hound of heaven. But people petted him down small and quiet, cultivated him. He fits into their church.

I heard someone crying *God,* in a broken voice. I saw someone else muttering. I asked him, "What are you muttering about, there?" He said, "I'm praying to God." But neither of them could tell me whether he had ever received an answer. "Then why do you both keep calling upon him?" I asked. They both answered, "Keeping quiet is even worse."

A third one said to me, "*God?* Just an old word I learned and used to sing when I was real little. It still festers somewhere in my memory: *God Almighty, creator of heaven and earth.* He had a son, too, like some kind of ghost story. Just recently, it suddenly all came back, at my mother's funeral. I think it was hearing those old hymns again."

And still another told me, "I don't know why I'm living. I'm topsy-turvy; I don't know whether I'm walking or crawling, standing up or going in circles. But there's got to be an *answer* somewhere that will free me, some compassion that will bear me up. I feel like there must be someone deep inside me, living and giving me life. I can't help but think this; with every breath I'm breathing it: *somewhere, there's someone.* He's the one I mean when I say *God.*" Then it occurred to me: *he?* why not *she?*

Someone says, "God doesn't exist." I ask him, "What do you mean by *exist,* and who or what do you mean by *God?*" He says, "So you think that God really does exist?" I ask him, "What do you mean by . . ." etc. He says, "So you think . . ." etc. Et cetera.

I said, "There is no God because people are so bad." Someone heard me, walked right up to me and said, "Okay, so there is no God. But there's me, right here." And he treated me just as though I were his friend. After a long time I began to think, "Well, perhaps there's at least someone who is not so bad."

Someone, outside, over against me.
To know someone: to be known, for a moment.
To do someone justice: to be someone yourself.

Known: no longer enough for myself; not to be able
to be thought away; indispensable.
Known: not overwhelmed, not almost defaced,

not dazzled blind; but gentled and touched.
Love. Beloved light. Sun breaking through mist,
carefully, covering me, with respect.

Heard: not drowned in dead silence;
fathomed patiently.
Tried: am I real, of the stuff of him
who said: I am?

Seen: by him, who said: Let there be light.*
Nobody can prove it, but you know when you are seen.
The psalms, Jesus, an age-old, defenseless,
hidden faith — these come to the aid
of my wavering feeling of happiness.

Known is known; death cannot change it.

The 70's. God is still there; he's there again. Death was
only apparent. Only a synonym for "far away," "holy,"
"eternal," "unspeakable." God is *dead* really meant, on
second thought and a bit more reflection, divinely dead,
more-than-living.

It worked well, saying, "He is dead." It shocked, gained
publicity, spurred people to take a stand, personally. What
a lot of talking then, high and low—and praying! Especially among ordinary people. Of course, the influx of
Eastern religions should not be overlooked.

The death of God did not last long, fortunately. After
only eight years or so, he emerged from the discussion,
exonerated and good as new. We can't bear to think, "Suppose he had not?" But he has, in fact, survived all the theologians, that God.

We are grateful that he's back again. Down deep, we
really knew it all along, knew he would come back, that
he is ineradicable.

Welcome back, God! We greet Thee, or rather you, a
jolly good fellow. From now on you shall have your regular

place once more, right in our midst. Which nobody can deny, which nobody can deny.

∾ SONG (a round)

text & inscription: H. Oosterhuis
tr: R. McGoldrick
music: Orlando di Lasso (16th century)

Tekening: Nout Verhoeven

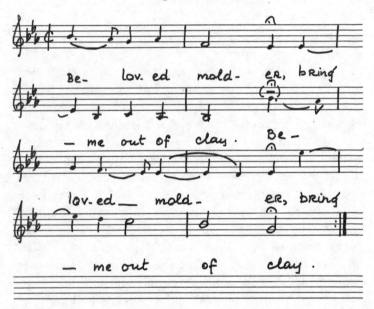

∾ SON OF

Talking about God is water that has flowed together out of clear and muddy springs. From under a rock, out of the clouds. Out of little faucets that insist on never being quite shut off but steadily drip and drip.

My faucet connects to a loose, shaky pipe which connects to a pump in a small pond (somewhere in a monastery garden) which connects with a canal which connects with the branch of a river which flows into the sea.

As it is written: he was now, for good, the son of Toon, son of Hendrik, son of Tjeerd Pieter postman in Uithuizen c. 1850, son of Pieter Tjeerd, son of . . . , then a stretch of years, feast and famine, son of Claus customs officer in the region of Bedum 1678, a bastard they say of the bishop of Munster, son of milking and mowing, son of sailing homecoming and off again, son of shouts words songs ("a mighty fortress"), son of sighs "alle dinghe sijn mi te inghe":* I find all things too narrow, son of restless my heart until . . . , son of why hast thou forsaken me, son of Joseph people say, son of Jacob, son of Matthan, son of son of son, dust of dust, twilight of twilight, evil out of good out of evil out of worse, son of David, son of Judah, son of Jacob Israel ("battle with God"), son of Isaac (whom the knife nearly got), son of Sarah's barren womb, son of Terah dealer in gods, son of Serug, son of the slave of the servant of the son of the lord of the tower of Babel, son of Shem, son of Noah, son of Giants, son of Enoch who was so kind he didn't have to die—no one has seen him since

that was when the last lunar volcanoes had already been extinguished for a thousand million years, in brief of Jared and of Kenan and Enosh, son of Seth ("in place of Abel"), son of Adam, son of you.

❧ SONG AT THE FOOT OF THE MOUNTAIN *

(melody: psalm 68, Geneva Psalter)

You, naming you is all in vain
no road can reach your far domain
nor any word adore you.
You, not up there enthroned on high
but light that dims in cloudy sky
or tale of vanished glory.
You come, we know not day nor hour
you pass nearby, a breath of fire
a stillness through trees streaming.
Crying far-off yet near us, too
not here nor everywhere are you
not that god we keep dreaming.

No nice safe path to walk along
no spot or leg to stand upon
no rock, no firm foundation.
No heart that speaks, no spurting springs
no blood that wells and swells and sings
no soul for contemplation.
No neat round number, standard rule
no doomsday hanging over all
in dire and dreadful fashion.
But you are people maimed and small
the homeless nameless people—all
who cry out for compassion.

Resounding stillness, voice-so-thin
if you exist, exist in them

in people all around us.
If you are not and cannot be,
elusive word, come be in me
no god we make an idol.
You know me and you bind me tight
I cry out you both day and night
and cannot quite forget you;
how then could we be I-alone
be homeless nameless and forlorn
and yet not know each other?

❧ THE FLUTE-PLAYER

The brass flute in the early morning, the voices of day-break. He opened his eyes and saw that it was beautiful. But no one else saw it, only he, he alone.

"Who is playing the flute?" he asked his mother. She didn't know. He went on listening, for a long time.

"Who is playing the flute?" His father didn't know, either. "Daddy is so dumb," thought the little boy, "I'm going to find out!" He cleaned up his plate, and set out upon the road.

"Cross over the mountains," said the road. "I'll carry you over." He walked all day through the mountains, but he did not find him. It grew dark.

Meanwhile, his father and mother could not hold back their tears. But the little boy went on thinking, "Daddy is so dumb. Why didn't he know?"

The next day, there it was again, the brass flute in the early morning.

"He'll never come back," people told his father. "He must have drowned in the sea, or something. Too bad, but that's how it goes."

Years later, he did come back, found the house of his father and mother standing empty, and moved in.

"You're not the one," everybody said. "You drowned in the sea, that's for sure." He was silent.

"You pretend that you've found him," people sneered, "but it's been a long, long time since you even existed— that's one thing we're sure of!"

They spat on him, as he passed by.

The very next day—the brass flute in the early morning.

But no one else heard it, only he, he alone.

❧ IF YOU HAD BEEN

O God O Lord of hosts
and our belovéd Lord,

if you had been
a bird this winter
migrant on the long trek south
among ten thousand others
you would have been
snared in a swishing net
captured killed and sold;
and of an evening out with friends
I'd get you on my plate
à l'orange or something,
sixteen guilders and a half
for your leg and a piece
of your wing.

if you had been
a baby seal
or other treasured beast—

perhaps a pheasant on the dunes of Wassenaar—
by now you would have
had it.

if you had been
a Rhenish fish
or just a rose
at the mouth of the Rhine
you would not be
you would be done for
long ago;
no fish swarm there
the roses do not climb there
any more.

O God O Lord of hosts
and our belovéd Lord.

if you had been a heron, you would have been
run over on the recent road through Flevoland.
if you had been a child, you soon could not
play anywhere in Holland anymore.

if you had been Moroccan
here in Amsterdam
in a boardinghouse
seven beds to a room
twelve by twelve

you would be up in flames.

❧ WHEN I WAS A CHILD

1.
I dream a meadow with live wires around it.
in armor midst the anonymous faces
I stand, with all my hair cut off. he looks
coldly past my gaze. where then my exile?

2.
Ice Age. glassy sea like frozen womb. I
skate for my life, and hardly make the turn.
with burning head I hold beneath my burden.
I have seen fire. seen him. and have not died.

❧ HE IS FRIEND

He does not punish. Whoever is not good punishes, and
must punish. Evil is self-punishing. People, being power-
less, punish each other. But he is more human than people.
He knows. He sees more. And he makes things new. *God
is friend; we are strangers* (Eckhart, 13th century).

He rewards? He is not my Lord and Master. He really does
not exercise power, does not give me orders. He rewards
as friends reward each other—with friendship. And friendship cannot be paid for; it is forever owing to the other.

Did he create me? Rather, we create each other, in the way
that friendship makes me *me* and you *you,* makes us each
other (who is changed into whom?).

He doesn't want to be propitiated, avenged, or to see blood. He wants to be known, to see you.

He cannot do all things. He cannot make you other than my neighbor. He cannot forgive me the wrong I do to you, nor can he forgive me if I refuse to forgive you. He cannot make me other than your neighbor.

God is simply of no *use*. Things go better without him: making headway with a woman, making money or poems, walking on the moon. Takes less time. Nor does he ease death off your shoulders. You don't really get anything out of him. He does not fulfill your longing. He just makes it worse.

To have God. To have need, now or later; a card up your sleeve, a defense. To hold him dear, as one usually holds children: in order to be loved and indispensable. (The eternal dream: "God has need of me.") That is human, "religion." To greet him for nothing, to name God for nothing, because he *is* no-thing, is God. To desire nothing of him, no self-awareness, no *I*-dentity, *no merit, no honor, no holiness, no heaven* (Eckhart)—that is to pray. That is the fruit of friendship.

Does God exist? Numbers exist, as does zero, and the hobbits. Alice exists in Wonderland. The world exists (so far). You exist—you can't help it, obviously. All things *are:* here, or there, evident, necessary, de facto. But is God a "thing"? Is he a "fact"? Is he here or there? Or everywhere-nowhere? Is his name No-One, Not-God, Not-Existent? *Nothing present to God dies; everything becomes alive in him* (Eckhart, again).

To go to one's death: to go to him. To be hidden in his "non-existable" heart. No longer to wander in this shadow-realm, behind glass, under wraps, unknown. He is friend.

God was walking around the universe. All the solar systems and the nebulous stars ran under his feet like a field. Then he found a treasure, lying hidden in the field. It was this earth, with a man on it. And in his joy, he sold all that he had, his omnipotence and his all-seeing eye, his heaven and his hell, and bought the earth.

❧ THE GENT IN THE STREET

There is a man goes round our town,
round our town, round our town,
his heart is an enormous hole—
do you know his name?

There all the birds go flying in,
flying in, flying in,
there all the people are snared in—
I know his name. (do you?)

He dawdles and drifts
and splashes and swirls,
rides the wind through the streets
and grabs what he can
skylarks, sparrows
you and you
and everyman.

He took my father recently,
father mine, father mine,

and soon my son must go along,
since he thinks that's fun. (ha)

No one knows when he may come
like a thief who steals your heart;
"Rest in peace now, in the ground,"
he says when he comes. (who, me?)

O is there, then, no maid or man,
sturdy maid, handsome man,
who can escape this gentleman
or buy him off? (just try)

He dawdles and drifts
and splashes and swirls,
rides the wind through the streets
and grabs what he can
skylarks, sparrows
fishes, foxes
you and you
and everyman.

O to live yet for a while,
yet for a while, and one more while,
there are still many wondrous things
and I am still so young. (well)

I have many songs to sing,
songs to sing, songs to sing,
since the dead no longer sing,
dead folk are so sad.

So, people, look for someone else,
another and another one,

to share your life and share your dream,
and to share your death. (ah)

For one alone can only weep,
quietly weep, weep aloud,
and two are better than just one,
surely when it's cold. (brr)

He dawdles and drifts
and splashes and swirls,
he kicks and he snickers
and he keeps coming on,
rides the wind through the streets
and grabs what he can
skylarks, sparrows
fishes, foxes
giants, roses
you and me
and everyman.

JET-BLACK

Jet-black grows the light
dark as earth the sun
the moon, the stars.

Leaden hang the clouds
rain gone, it does not clear.

The caretaker flees, and the house
is left to stand unguarded.

Men strong as trees
tremble like reeds.

The hard hand of the miller's wife
is tired of milling.

Listless the whores
laughing behind their windows.

Doors are made fast for the night
the curtains are drawn
and are not opened again.

Toneless drones the voice of a singer
thin is the call of a bird.

    "Every height is too high
    the steps are too steep
    talking too hard"
    someone says,
    "I don't dare to go out
    in the frightening streets
    anymore."

"Olive trees, you delight me no more;
almond trees, bloom not for me."

"I cling to you still but feel you no more"
somebody says to another.

"Go, go to your lasting home"
the grave diggers cry through the streets,
"On to our final dwelling"
cry the dead to those still alive.

The silver cord is severed now
the golden lamp lies broken on the floor.

The jar cracks on the edge of the well
the waterwheel lifts no water on high—
only the silt-covered shells.

Dust to dust and earth to earth
all returns to its source again.

Our breathing flows toward the breathing sea,
toward him who lives.

after Ecclesiastes 12

❧ ABC's

A: "Though my body is broken, though my heart dies,
   you are my rock, my God, the future that awaits me."
   Numberless people, when dying, have said these words
   from psalm 73.
B: To whom?
C: There have been, and there always are, even more peo-
   ple who couldn't manage to get the words out, living
   or dying. It never even enters their heads.
A: A psalm that has survived for twenty-five centuries.
B: Lust and unfaithfulness have survived for a hundred
   centuries.
A: Lust and unfaithfulness are no wonder. These words
   are. They wouldn't exist if they had not been lived.
C: They come from fear. People who live in fear, die in
   fear.
A: These are last words. Too big for a book. They come

already from the other side. Someone trying to say, in vague, broken language, hardly clear to himself or anybody else, something he has actually lived . . . and—

B: *wished* he had lived

C: and halfway through, his voice breaks off and turns into a death rattle.

B: The words survive just because they have not been lived. They come from regret and guilt-feelings.

C: and they are unlivable. They're determined to live them, all the dying, but they don't.

A: They're determined to live them, all the dying, and they do, and more than that.

B: You talk as though you have been dead and have come back to life again.

C: Let's drop it. You can't dispute words like those; they're like anything else you can't grapple with. God himself is not arguable. It makes no sense to reason about whether he exists, and how, or not. Why would someone dispute whether God exists, if he already knows there is no God?

❧ SONG OF THE DEAD

Like ships come out of no man's land
    propelled across the water
and weathering both calm and storm
    at last sunk in the harbor,

like leaning houses so worn out
    not even squatters live in,
the floors and old supports in ruins
    roof weather-beaten, riven,

so deep the deaf and sunken dead
    now buried in their furrows,
ploughed under, fertilized, they sprout
    no sprigs, no green tomorrows.

Or under some undreamed of sun
    transformed — are they tall oak trees?
or maybe mine shafts full of gold
    forgotten in the Rockies?

Or do they fly before the dawn,
    turned into great white heron,
no longer human beings now?
    how can we hope to learn?

We flow and no one knows to where,
    dry up in autumn canyons;
becalmed and cold in every bone,
    we go without companions.

DEAD LETTER

How much longer?
Have you simply banished me from your thoughts?
No?
But you sure try.
I hear you're doing badly,
that you're nowhere.
How long will you go on
avoiding me
or passing by in disguise
or not answering when I phone
not opening when I knock?

Must that go on,
this discord in my soul
this suffocating doubt—
never again . . . but still?
And the neighbors and our close friends
who know about us
just laugh and say
"him and his God!"
While people treat me
like gods, still
no word from you, and even
this letter is not deliverable.
And some fine day
we're going to die, with a plop
or slowly of a tumor
or drift away in sleep.
Standing over me
that single foe shall bend,
the deadly enemy.
I'll feel his breath
upon my face
and then I'll barely hear him saying:
finally.

Even then I'll cling to you
whether you want me or not,
in your good grace
or out of it.
"Save me!" I'll cry out to you
or maybe only
"Love me."

psalm 13, freely adapted

❧ OF SWIMMING AND SAILING

Lemmings are little rodents, found in northern Europe and Siberia. They belong to the *vole* genus. At long, unpredictable intervals, they trek seaward in enormous numbers, plunge into the waves, and swim out until all of them drown.

One day, a hundred years ago, somewhere in the Brazilian jungle, a small tribe of Indians who were nearly extinct (and nearly domesticated), abandoned their tents, their strips of land along the river, and their dark haunts in the swampland. Fires were extinguished, axes buried. They took nothing with them. Up and gone, eastward where the sun climbs up the sky, onward toward the seacoast.

"We are going," they told their children, "to God."

They trekked on, for a month, a whole season. They crossed the last mountain. There was the sea.

No God to be seen.

They descended the last slope of the mountain, stumbled across the rocky beach, and walked into the sea. The water rose to their waists, to their necks. They just had time to call out to each other "Here we go!"

One by one, they disappeared beneath the water, the children first.

The fishermen stepped into the boat and rowed out on the lake. It grew dark, and he had still not come to them. The water turned very rough and a strong wind arose.

When they had rowed about three miles, they saw him coming toward them, walking upon the water. Panic seized them. But he said to them, "It is I, do not be afraid."

He stepped into the boat, and they reached the coast they were bound for.

He is a dusky
patch in the darkness,
trace of moisture
still on the ground.
He is the whirlwind
he moves around
turning, creeping
standing
walking upright.

Swimming and sailing
walking into the waves
walking and walking
over the sea.

Planting and waiting
spinning and stitching
luring birds into
cages, and more—
pulling trees up
wrestling with giants
hunting and killing—
man can do these.

Swimming and sailing
walking into the waves
walking and walking
over the sea.

Building houses
keeping the rain out,
gifted with speaking
he is in luck;
joins in with others,

he can think, also
only death
was not his idea.

Swimming and sailing
walking into the waves
walking and walking
over the sea.

He is inventive
nerves made of steel
always enduring—
man can do these;
laughing, weeping
curing diseases
only death
he cannot cure.

Swimming and sailing
walking into the waves
walking and walking
over the sea.

He can imagine
a mouse or a mountain
he's good at playing
and sometimes he sees;
carping, singing
high jumper, broad jumper
only death
he cannot outjump.

Swimming and sailing
walking into the waves
walking and walking
over the sea.

Two times one
and that makes two
hearts exchanging . . .
(only death)
flying, fleeing
from each other
only death
they cannot flee.

Swimming and sailing
walking into the waves
walking and walking
over the sea.

It cannot happen
yet it shall be,
two people standing
facing the night;
just for a moment
outrunning darkness
all of us standing
facing our death.

Swimming and sailing
walking into the waves
walking and walking
over the sea.

～ ABOUT THIS BOOK

A workbook. Made for one or another, to do something
with. No one excluded.
   Selections for use. Used selections: sung, spoken.

To be read slowly, better aloud, still better with ten or a thousand together. Don't just skim over the lines, please.

Written to hold fast to something, to discover anew. A book like a ritual. A book to pray—one man's ecstasy written down, his delirium observed. This is what I wanted to do, have tried to do; what, between laughter and tears, I have heard and seen.

Fragments. Remnants?
Fragments—now, snapshots, sketches on a journey.
Who knows more and will teach me? Who throws a stone at my glass house?
  A few more questions: who? what? why? what do you believe in, then? a different way? no way? out in the cold? been disillusioned? never thought about it? want to, maybe? sure of that?

Epigraph for this book—
at times we see further than we are.

ᴥ DEAD IS DEAD
(notes for a TV script about people)

The villagers send out five young men to fight the possessed swine that run around in their mountains, destroying their vineyards. After weeks of hunting and slaughtering, they return, one pig-eared, another with a snout, the third bulging with bacon fat, the fourth with flapping teats, the fifth grunting and smeared with mud. The villagers seize their sticks, drive the five of them out of the village, up into the mountains, and there they slaughter them.

Tekening: Nout Verhoeven

The scene is Amsterdam, and you don't know anybody there. Beautiful big city, but there's nothing doing. Me in my best suit, what am I doing here? Young people, all kinds, all around, and me—a divorced man. And you really don't have any neighbors.

What a blindingly beautiful little mask you're wearing.

One can't very well go out alone. So you look for someone to take you out, now and then, maybe to a cabaret. Sometimes you answer one of those ads. You can never tell, even though, so far . . . You're just looking for some human companionship, and what do you get? They all think: after all, nobody answers one of those things without knowing the score.

Everybody seeks his own. His own millstone. His own gamble.

Once in a while, you just have to talk. Maybe just one hour in the whole long day. But to whom? I've done it to the walls. To myself. I just want to hear my own voice, once in a while.

Without realizing it, he had gradually given up all hope that his life would ever make any sense.

For forty years now, with eyes wide open, he has never seen me.

My one leg is stiff. My cane is broken. My chauffeur is moody, and my husband is, too. My daughter shacks up and my son smokes pot. I sleep badly, yet I keep growing older—the last straw!

I cut wood for my neighbor's furnace. I don't sleep with my neighbor's wife. And I say things, at times, which nearly kill me.

Something you didn't want to happen sometimes proves, later, to be good, very good.

He didn't care who he beat up, as long as he was beating up somebody. That was all he cared about.*

He always said, "War and sex are all that matters. I stick to that. Life depends on chance and hormones, it's not worth talking about."

— I've never thought about dying.
— When I die, I'm not simply gone. I'd want to know the *why* of everything, or at least my own why.
— Right now we're alive. We belong to each other, period.
— I'd like to be a person with no walls around me.
— Look, we find it nice being together. Let's just work at that, as our goal.
— I'd like to be enlightened. I'm not quite sure what I should believe in.
— Just believe in me.

"Then you want to say everything, and you can't say anything. Yet you have to say something."

"but I have to . . . I can't stand the sight of blood . . . listen, I wanna see some money . . . *you*, always *you*, it's your own fault . . . you sound half dead."

"You really should expect things like that in life, but somehow you never do."

I just laugh about it now, and don't get involved. To tell the truth, the whole thing leaves me cold now. I used to knock myself out, between the neighborhood action-groups, the discussion groups, and what-not, back in the 'sixties. Now, I can do without all those doubts, mistakes, risks. No, I have a good life here. No one knows me here.

That's one of the advantages of moving into a brand-new apartment building.

"Blood is so cheap. Everywhere."

> Man is man
>   and money might
> winter summer
>   day and night
> fair and foul
>   dark and light—
> it's the top
>   or bottom.
>
> Save your skin
>   I'll save my bread
> God is God
>   and dead is dead—
> it's the top
>   or bottom.

— But we were always so happy.
— You said that.

We reach out for the wall like people blinded,
    as though we had no eyes we grope ahead
stumbling at high noon as if in darkness
    we are in the waste land of the dead. (*Isaiah 59:10*)*

— That "Voice" must be too pure for my ears. I hear nothing.
— What don't you hear?
— And besides, nobody listens anyhow.
— Some people listen.
— I don't see a single one.

They sit on an island, a hundred thousand people. Slowly, the ice cap melts at the north pole, and the sea rises and rises, everywhere.

"We must throw up a dike," all the papers clamor, "to save ourselves."

When the forests have been cut down and the mountains leveled off to build the dike, there is still a great gap where plenty of water can come in. So everyone gives whatever he is willing to part with, to fill in the gap. Refrigerators, automobiles, bedclothes, earrings, old bibles—all are plunked down into the gap, until it is closed. And one December night, the wind and the sea pounce upon the dike.

SONG FOR SLAVES AND PRISONERS

They sang their song
half song and half a curse
(they knew tomorrow would be worse)
"no one came to save us."

"Each other's underlings, imprisoned in our dreaming,
longing for the fleshpots—such are we,
in dread of spiders and the dark, our hands
deploy odd bits of fluff, form rows of puppets
armed to the teeth or, as hamsters keep rounding
glass cages, so do we."

They sang their song
half song and half a curse
(they knew tomorrow would be worse)
"no one came to save us."

"If we dream of swimming, happy
in a river swift with sun,
we are only dry-gilled fish, remains of fins
in a pond dried up and choked with dancing weeds.
Would it were different, but we're not meant to journey,
wingless and not set to travel."

They sang their song
half song and half a groan
(they knew no future, no way home)
"no one came to save us."

"No one keeps watch or ventures forth
to hear a voice, perhaps to gain an insight.
This lasts so long, expands like air
that's pumped in every head till all your brains
are numb and no one knows what
hope is now or wants a change, no one."

They sang their song
half song and half a cry
what future now have you and I?
no one came to save us.

p.s. A song for slaves and prisoners? Beautiful pathos, an
endearing little fiction. True, slaves groan; but sing?
Hardly. Their mouths have been stopped, with fists, and
they are not inclined to visions. Yet sometimes some of
them let out sounds like singing, cry out "We shall be . . .
free!" Let them alone. They're just homesick, just humming prayers set to harmless music.

❧ THE WORLD OF THE GODS

When there was no way
when there was no other way
than waging war;

when photos appeared in the papers
of those mass graves
and new strong men
and how the victor dubbed his cigarette
on the cheek of the vanquished,
when our guilder was still there
worth exactly a guilder
and evening came, and morning;

when we were still there, too
and everything was going just fine

"and gudrun begat baldur
and baldur begat menhir
and menhir begat mathilda
and mathilda begat mickey mussolini
and mussolini begat airwick
and airwick begat egbert roadbuilder
and egbert roadbuilder begat mae west
and mae west begat onan

and thus it was good and thus all things became
nice and redundant: the warm were warmed,
the poor made poorer, the bony boned"*

when the universe whirled with gadgets and slogans,
the twilight of the gods,
justice and injustice blindly intertwined;

when the Axel-Springer combine was booming
and the *Telegraaf* was the biggest paper
in Holland;

when things were working well
when you could bank on it;

when no one could tell me what to do,
when I was writing this book;

when the earth belonged to a handful of robber barons
when Surinam was still not for the Surinamers
when Angola continued Portuguese;
when much still had to happen before . . .
when still there were giants upon the earth
and the Three Sisters and iron-fisted mothers;

when rocks and craters were not yet
changed to fields and lakes;

when they had no more hope
when they had no more desires
when they thought: "we don't have any choice,"
"too bad," "there, there,"
when they said:
"we cannot do otherwise,"
"where would we be, otherwise?"

when people were silent, out of powerlessness
out of shame, out of respect, out of fear

out of boredom, embarrassment, not caring
out of compassion, out of calculation, out of contempt;

the silent majority

when there was no way, anymore, as yet
when it was so long since a third World War was not
    going on
when the end had not yet come
but was already well in sight;

when there was simply no place to begin
so vast was the world—
a sea of people;

when indeed the world existed
but was wild and desolate,

then

❧ HE'LL FIX THEM
(*an adaptation of psalm 12*)

Trust is gone
and unfeigned friendship.
Lost forgotten denied
that a man is a man
a word a word.
None unimpeachable
nothing sound
no shoulder firm.
Anxious lies, well-intentioned,
calculated, flattering—
that's our line.

He'll fix them,
double-talkers braggarts
carving up the world.
He'll tear out the tongues
cut off the lips of those who boast:
"my mouth is a knife,
my tongue a Wehrmacht,
my words a curtain of fire"—
ah gentlemen,
don't let him hear you.

He says,
"I cannot stomach any more of it,
the regular round of general slaughter,
the groaning of defenseless people.
I come."

His word is no word
of people;
it is attainment, tried
by despair and having to watch,
by endurance and endless
forgiving and hoping.

His word acts,
knows no yielding,
unmasks,
cries out to every person:

"What's your lie,
who are you?"

❦ WHO IS *I*?

There is a story which plays a quite active part in this world of strophic *when's,* in this world of lies begot by fear and self-interest, this world of gods. And it has retained that part even till today, as though its successive narrators formed an unbreakable chain linking all the ghettos and gas chambers of history. Of that story, the story of Israel, psalm 12, is but a fragment, a cry from the heart, the echo and impassioned voice of her whole history.

Israel's story tells us what anybody can know, what everybody in fact does know quite well, however deformed and stifled conscience may be, however drowned out or warped by words. People *know* that our world, with its regular round of general slaughter and groaning human beings, is simply not human, simply a non-world, a dark and eerie chaos like that which preceded those very first pronouncements: *light, man, you.* Because everybody is created with that conscience, endowed with it.

The story of Israel does not deny the facts, past or present, or argue them away, or flee from them or gloss over them. It provides no handy directions about how to live with them, how to become resigned to them—the way so many sacred stories, and perhaps all myths and systems of philosophy, have tried to do. Psalm 12 cries out, even screams, in the face of the facts—but it never flies in their face. Its whole burden is to spot and to unmask the "given" facts: Who gives them? To whom? What does "given" mean? And it unmasks them as *injustice.* It tells us their meaning, unsparingly; tells us what's really going on;

brings to light—*reveals*—what just blindly "happens" to be the "case": the majority of human beings simply *lack the means* to live decent human lives. *That* is the "given" fact.

And every human conscience is called to account for it.

But the story does even more. It asserts that justice is possible, that the last word shall not belong to the super-powers who divide up the world, to the mighty, to the gods. It says: there is someone who stands behind the poor and the dispossessed; there is a last judgment; there is a first Name; there is Someone there.

People, the story of Israel says, are not machinery doomed to grind on with mounting havoc, not the feckless playthings of fate. Someone with a heart has a plan, a purpose for people: they exist, by right and in freedom, in order to serve one another.

That Someone is the *I* in psalm 12. He is the one who cannot be named—*naming you is all in vain*—who rejects being idol or image; no "god," no power which oppresses and maims. He is only a voice which cries out to people: *where is your brother?* But that voice reaches to the very core of the earth, like a roaring fire.

He could be silent no longer, the story continues. When he saw that no one stood behind his people, no one; speechless that no one even wanted to help them, *then* he girded himself like a partisan, a guerilla. Not in priestly garments or liturgical vestments did He come, not equipped with a stethoscope or robed like a judge, but dressed for battle, wearing armor, an aroused and shaken God, prepared to go the limit. There is in his voice the unmistakable note caught by slaves and prisoners. It rings through the psalms, and in the songs of prophets.

When he saw that nobody was doing anything for his people, he himself leapt in, right into the midst of that curtain of fire, of argument and reasoning, with all its deadly rounds: *beyond a shadow of a doubt!* and *come on, answer the question!* and *but then come up with some practical alternative to our present capitalist system! (and if you do, I'm damn sure it'll be Commie to the core!)* Yes, in the midst of the stockholders' meeting, before that impressive assemblage of gods, super-powers, and developed (wealthy) countries, the voice of psalm 12 cries out:

Enough. I cannot stomach any more of it. Your great economic processes—your flawless machinery of forces and counter-forces, your tidy family tree of cause-and-effect (airwick begat egbert roadbuilder/ and egbert roadbuilder begat mae west/ and mae west begat onan*)—your whole tree spreads out at-the-cost-of at-the-cost-of at-the-cost-of another family tree, groaning under-the-weight-of helpless-masses-of butchered-human-beings! And it goes on-and-on, slyly, invisibly, matter-of-factly, amid *who can say who is to blame?* and *who can interrupt the course of history, realistically speaking?*

The voice of psalm 12 replies: I can. I want to be the voice of your conscience, once more.

The story of Israel is the story of that voice. And the voice says:

the earth does not belong to a handful of rulers,
but to everyone who lives upon it.

poverty is theft.

hunger is theft.

thou knowest how the great ones of the earth
lord it over the small;
let it not be so among you.

thou shalt not exploit nor belittle the stranger
in thy midst.

thou shalt not allow anyone to slave for thee—
thou hast been, remember,
both slave and stranger thyself.

whoever has taken a coat from another as security,
when the cold of the evening comes
let him give it back.
it is the only covering such a man has
for his naked body.
otherwise, how shall he be able to go to sleep?

no one is god—I alone,
but that doesn't matter
it is not a question of me.
what matters is
the poor, the refugee
the orphan, the widow
those who are dying by the wayside.
they are the touchstones
they are "god."

fear not—for no one is god.
all those gods and powers,
they are not inescapable
not decreed by nature
not eternal laws
not last judgments.
they are, after all, only people
they can be unmasked
they can be conquered—fear not.

and these words I have spoken to you,
inscribe them upon your hearts
upon your dining room tables
upon your doorposts.
mark your foreheads with them and burn them into the
palms of your hands.

He made a beginning with them, says the story of Israel.
Deep in history, before there was a "history," when there
was only unchangeable fate, a rock-bound status quo, the
everlasting turning of the same old wheel—cruelty, violence, blood-drenched reprisals, and always and again "the
poor made poorer"—when we were brutal and primitive,
not yet human—he made a beginning, with us.

And when the voice had spoken, people began to come out
of those corners where blows are always falling, those caves
and crannies, people began to come to light. Most of them
dragged their feet. And most of them crawled quickly back
again.

  Rather, most of them (three-fourths of the world's pop-
ulation?) just stood there, motionless, a huge, harmless,
faceless mass of people known as "the poor." No one need
be frightened in their presence; it never occurs to them
that the world might be other than it is. As Bertolt Brecht
says of them,

> They no longer respond,
> they stand like sticks
> someone has randomly
> stuck in the sand;
> if you wave them away,
> at once they are gone.
> Nothing perturbs them now.
> Only at the scent of food
> do they raise their eyes.*

But a handful of them stumbled along in the direction of the voice, following behind it—and that, then, is known as "the exodus" in the story of Israel. Turks and Moroccans who clean our restaurants, deep in the night, who mop the floors of our banks and perhaps pave our highways —all of them, sooner or later, stand up and say *No, we take no more of this*. The exodus. From the foundries and furnaces of Egypt, says that story, he has led you into the desert, just with his voice, into that desert wherever slaves and prisoners get themselves, singly and collectively, together. And there, in that desert, the grumbling starts, the loud complaints, the storm of cries and curses, of terrifying dreams. As happens—with people continuously and deeply provoked.

And there they come to regret their exodus, for sand is sand and not bread. There, at times, they are subject to mirages, or to a sudden burst of song, to visions—like water spurting out of dry rock.

There, too, begins the whole conversation, deliberation, confused analyzing of the old days, what things were like "when we still believed in all that idolatrous machinery." There the place for deep reflection, for meetings, brainstorming, evaluating "data," the laborious planning sessions to come up with something new, the endless experimenting to come up with justice for all. There in the desert, where perhaps one is reduced at last to real words, unfeigned friendship, integrity.

And the voice, where is it to be heard?

In your conscience?

In a psalm, in the story of Israel, in that outlandish, enigmatic book?

In this or that new law which is, perhaps, not quite as bad as the old one?

In some vision of the future which, here and there, some-one stammers out?

In people?

Are there quite sane people who know, for certain, that the voice speaks and is trustworthy? Who know that things will be turned inside out and upside down, that the hungry shall be fed, and the last shall be first, even if it takes, let us say, ten thousand years?

It will never happen, smile the gods.

It certainly will, some day—who says this? Who? I?

YE GODS *

High and mighty
indestructible
in your black abysmal light
inaccessible
sealed and air-tight
on your leaden thrones;
who would dare not grovel
when he greets you?

you with ears
that do not hear
and mouth that never speaks

Gods of money
you are dog-eared
as old dollars
gilt-edge cash;
you're the banker in the game
you short-change every time,
you pulverize

the cricket and the fly
between your paws

you with ears
that do not hear
and mouth that never speaks

Your alabaster nose
smells nothing,
your fingers
hard as diamonds
have no choice, no chance;
no hope for you
no maybe's
no godknows,
you stand in stone
and all your dreams are straw

you with ears
that do not hear
and mouth that never speaks

But I am other
I am counter,
unpredictable,
an uprooted clod of grass
trailing bits of earth,
I am water
in your iron-gloved hand
and slip between your fingers
slip away
into the sand

you with ears
that do not hear
and mouth that never speaks

and I who disappear.

I slip and slide
between the pebbles
am ground by boulders,
scoured clean and flayed,
search on
impelled
beyond the hound and hunter

become a spring
a dauntless river
and new life

you with ears
that do not hear
and mouth that never speaks

and I who live anew,
reborn—no thanks to you!

✒ THERE HAVE BEEN PEOPLE

Large is the world
and time is long
but small the feet
that go where no roads go—
go everywhere.

A round I wrote. A riddle? Has it ever happened, have
there ever been people who have gone where no roads go?

The story of Israel describes, with significant detail, how
people really are, how imprisoned, how addicted to their

imprisonment. It tells how, for sheer self-preservation, people—in the long run—begin to worship the very powers who have brought them to their knees. How, crazed by this long run, they are doomed to starve and massacre each other—and this in the name of their tyrants. So it goes, on and on, in every concentration camp, 1973 years after Christ and at least 1973 years before Christ. Their aggressions will always implode, their guilt feelings, carefully sown and cultivated, will destroy the last remains or the first seeds of their longing for freedom. They will begin to think that they are not worthy of freedom (and we, the slave drivers, will continue, quite untroubled by them). After a while, they won't even know any more that they *are* imprisoned, or that there are fellow-prisoners, fellow-victims, allies.

Just try to tell the Bible, that book with no illusions, something about people!

There have been people, says the story of Israel, for whom the voice of conscience mattered above all else, for whom that voice was simply the most persistent voice in reality, the ineradicable sense of right and wrong. Whether from far or near, nothing they heard affected them as deeply as did that voice. In the moaning of masses of common people—three-fourths of the world—or in one lone person standing at their side or in front of them, they recognized the voice. They knew that to flee from that voice would be to flee from themselves.

There have been people who have said to the voice: you and you alone are our God. And they have been as good as their word. They have walked in his footsteps because they have wanted to be the followers and allies of him who had sworn by his right hand that he would not rest until justice should shine like the sun in the sky. "People who do not build their lives upon appearances, who do not make up lies against each other"—thus they are typified in psalm 24; people who hunger and thirst after justice, as they are called in that most impossible place in the gospels, the Sermon on the Mount. Whoever follows him will see him in the very following, gradually. Toiling and trudging along in his footsteps (in his spirit), they come to the light. It is while they are *doing* God that they see God.

There have been people who have offered themselves, in order to pass on the voice by this *doing* God. Because only those who live the story of Israel, and guarantee its credibility with their bodies, with their lives, only they pass that voice on. Everything they see, hear, think, dream presents itself against the background of that story. It is their vision of the future and their conscience.

There have been people who have known the worst—the curtain of fire, who have nothing to lose because they have nothing left, who have survived to the end, and have somehow survived the end. *Then* they set out. Their starting point is the absurd, that moment in which things could not be worse—death itself: "all trust gone . . . no shoulder firm" (psalm 12).

Are they blinded or just naive, in setting out? Can they no longer think straight? Doesn't even the most perfunctory analysis of human "reality" lead to the conclusion that we are, in fact, doomed to move in vicious circles, to efforts at escape that are futile and stillborn? Even so, they revise and survive their own analysis against the background of the vision, a vision no more demonstrable than the rightness of humor, and no less contagious and refreshing—because the vision is all they have, and because they are determined to survive.

At work in their vision like yeast is that memory . . . people who once set out, set out from death, crushed people who dared to get up and cry out, cries of birth. Their rising up was so irresistible that the whole earth trembled in crisis; says the story of Israel: "the mountains, like rams, began jumping; the sea took to flight." Then it was that those words were first spoken—"God himself went before them."

There have been such people. There still are. In them, one can verify the vision. People who undertake to vouch for the fact that an exodus, a new beginning, is perhaps something more than a mere mirage, after all.

No one trustworthy? No one who does justice? There have been, and there are, those who do justice, indeed. They themselves have become the story of Israel. They are that vision. The Bible says they really happened. That they are the deepest truth, their trustworthiness most worthy of trust in all of history. Unforgettable people. Their names are preserved: Abraham, Moses, Joshua, Jesus.

Look at them and do as they do. Go their way.
Who, me? Yes, you.

❦ WINTER SONG *

> no silvery sleigh bells
> no gold in the ground
> only a hand on my heart
> and a love I have found

> Winter time. on the beach. in shabby coats
> leaky shoes. ranged like dark pilings

branded with numbers. stoically standing
waiting on the beach. a winter day.

We look but do not see. there is no horizon.
a shadow flits nearby and lightly skims the water
a sea gull snatching fish out of the foam
gliding along the rolling whitecaps.

There are many of us on the beach
most of us tired and confused. worn out.
no longer knowing how to go on. cold and shelterless.
forsaken now the old land, the waste land.

   no silvery sleigh bells
   no gold in the ground
   only a hand on my heart
   and a love I have found

Rich and poor equal now equally beaten—
turtle and hare   the snake   the greyhound
the race is over at the water's edge
that sea which no one can leap over.

Go? who dares go? how do we go if we go?
who on one leg? who dares jump in headfirst?
who will dive in and swim beneath the breakers?
who will be tossed like a bottle on the sea?

Where to go? go naked or with clothes on?
perhaps like white dark-headed sea gulls
to glide along the surging crest of rolling waters
hoarsely outshouting the pounding breakers:

   no silvery sleigh bells
   no gold in the ground

only a hand on my heart
and a love I have found

Does anyone know the password or have a key?
or have any food? or a dream? a tender memory?
anyone still know that hymn "He Is My Shepherd"?
someone starts toward the water, starts the singing:

no silvery sleigh bells
no gold in the ground
only a hand on my heart
and a love I have found

Someone makes a start—perhaps a wolf or shepherd
or underbrush or oak or creeping vine.
a rosebush shakes itself and is but brambles
a youngster carries his father on his shoulders.

no silvery sleigh bells
no gold in the ground
only a hand on my heart
and a love I have found

Ten or twenty go, or one or maybe thousands
as if a song, as if the other shore were real
and death had died and sea had fled
with stinging salty waters—they all go singing:

I need no pathway
I need no key
no beautiful house
no silvery sleigh bells
no gold in the ground
only a hand on my heart
and a face turned to me

and a love I have found
and a harp and a flute
like a woman and man
and the steaming of mist
in the sun rising over
the new Vietnam.

no silvery sleigh bells
no gold in the ground
only a hand on my heart
and a love I have found.

THEN STEPPED THE STUMP

Then stepped the stump
half burnt
out of the fire, and went his way.
And the thistle crawled
out of sandy soil
and went his way.
They happened to meet
and soon agreed
to continue onward together.

They came upon an egg.
"Want to come?"
"I do!" said the egg.
They waded through a brook.
"Come on!"
"Okay!" said the brook
and rolled himself up like a curl.
The fishes, too, joined in
and so they came to a woods.

There dwelt a wolf.
"Come on!"
"Where to?" said the wolf.
The rambling rose
went also
and the snake from under his rock.
A real cortège
bobbing up and down
over meadows —
the turnip, too, the goat
the grass-fed lamb
the sweet pea in bloom, the dew
the pale bones of a giant
jumping up, and the jackknife
snapping open and swinging along.

By the moonlight
they took counsel now.
"Makin' good time,"
cried the egg, "but where to?"
"To the moon,"
offered the fishes.

But the wolf had a plan in store.

"Speak, dear wolf!" put in the lamb.
"Let's be people,"
said the wolf.
They all lay down now, two by two.
And the stump and the brook
together turned into a man;
then the sweet pea, the dew
and the snake and the egg
together turned into a man;
and the thistle and the fish

down the line, two by two
the rose and the knife
the wolf and the lamb.

Thus was it evening and morning.

❧ VOICE

Voice like a sea of people
round me, through my veins.
Voice of someone drowning—
the waterlogged remains
   of a man, I see,
    as·he looks at me.

Voice that cries: who are you,
and your brother—where is he?
Voice that breaks my fetal sac
and sets me free; that strikes
   a stone and makes fire fly,
    you who make me I.

Voice that has no name, as yet,
people who have no voice.
Voice like a woodpecker tapping
upon my inner ear.
   Word that resounds to the last,
    God—who holds me fast.

✎ THE NAME: An Agreement

Moving on, says the story of Israel, we have picked up the trail of his name (his "essence"): who he is in our regard, how he treats us, and how dependable and liberating that is. At this point we may call him: not-one-of-those-gods; not-a-god-like-those-other-gods.

"I am he who cries out to you" is his name. "I shall always be there, I shall always cry out to you" is his name. "As long as there are people, I shall cry out to you" is his name. "I am the poor" is his name.

"A God of the dark corners and crannies, the God of all the unhealthy neighborhoods of the world" sneers Nietzsche, on target.

This, all of it, is his name, once and for all.

"I shall have no other names," says the voice.

"I am the voice who cries out: *who are you?*" is his name.

"I am he who cries out: *where is your brother?*" is his name.

Name which is no name. No tidy formula at one's disposal, guaranteed to work. No code word which will do for "the concept of God"; no key word in some philosophical system.

Unspeakable name, name not to be said but to be *done*, name which becomes credible only in what I do, don't do. Or incredible.

Someone hearing even a single fragment of that story of Israel is bound to ask himself whether the voice of this poor man's God does not come through as an unceasing appeal to his conscience, and as an indictment of every "god" people have ever set before themselves.

Suppose that the biblical story which is told to me, translated for me, sung at me, quoted and explained to me finally makes me feel that the contemporary, established order of things (our kind of society, our brotherhood and human *being*) is, after all, better than I had thought; or suppose the biblical message I get reduces to "Well, you can't do anything about it, anyhow," or even blesses the "haves" (the Baal-gods), approves the smooth-talkers, and excuses the super-powers who divide up the world—then I know, I ought to know, I can and must know that it is *not* that unspeakable name which has been handed down to me.

It is hereby agreed: when we say, sing, swear, or think *God,* we mean that voice, that unspeakable name.

A clock stopped,
the door of thought
closed behind me.
Over the chasm
a singing bridge
descends.
Untangled, I turn back
to the softest spot
in my memory—
your name.

Your name is a shrivelled hand
a branch which does not bloom

a navel cord cut off
a pair of scissors.
All other gods are talking serpents,
palaces made of eyes;
your name is a modest cottage
thatched with pubic hair.
The names of other gods are mountains
spangled with flowers, islands
overgrown, forbidden sea lanes,
a beach of pearly shells.

Your name is a shadow upon the water,
a gust of dust, a little cloud
of sand kicked up.

Ever since you asked me
who I am and why,
I simply don't exist
any more
outside of you.

To think
I hardly knew your name
when you first asked me.

∾ PSALM 14
The fool says in his heart,
"There is no God."

Do-nothings, numbskulls, gods
the living dead are they
who claim,
    "your god is no god,

what he commands is crazy
half-baked and unfeasible."
Duds are they who say,
"there is no last judgment
no first name."
Their deeds are suited to their words:

they tear up the road
lay waste the land;
and no one knows the answer
no one does what is just
no one.

Vampires who suck our breath,
snouts rooting up the riches
out of other people's land,
they plant dragon's teeth and dreadful dreams
all around,
they snatch the struggling word
out of the mouth of the poor.

They tear up the road
they lay waste the land;
and no one knows the answer
no one does what is just
no one.

From his hidden place
out beyond our light
he keeps his eyes
hopefully turned
toward the children of men,
looking for one
even one anywhere

in whatever far corner
who knows better and starts in anew
one child who dares
one man who will stretch out his roots
toward the wellsprings.
But all are withered and stumped,
and no new start endures.

They tear up the road
they lay waste the land;
and no one knows the answer
no one does what is just
no one.

"Have they still never heard of me?"
he says,
"these contrivers of death
who squander my people,
eat them up like bread;
who deny that I am who I am
that I know by name
the least of the poor
that it is my name
to be God of the outcast
that however entrenched they may be, still . . .
my troth and my future
shall outlast them all.
If they knew that, they would surely
drop dead from fear."

They tear up the road
they lay waste the land;
and no one knows the answer
no one does what is just
no one.

Now they still have the power
to make fun of the poor
to make them ashamed
of their dream of a land of their own,
to shackle them so
they despair of the vision.

I, says the Lord
I shall do them justice.

   Do they tear up the road?
   Do they lay waste the land?
   I am he who knows the answer
   someone who does what is just
   someone.

Will salvation ever dawn for us,
the city of peace?
Will he order our fortune
for the best,
he who has said,
"I am your God
'your future' is my name"?
Can a whole people
ever rise up from the dead?

❦ THE POWER THAT WENT OUT FROM HIM *
Notes on Jesus of Nazareth

He is books, footnotes, sermons. A film. A cry on a
T-shirt. A crutch-word, like God. He finds a place in an
episcopal coat of arms, and in a song of Simon and Gar-

funkel (he "loves you more than you will know"). Organs
and candles, ailing animals and the crowns of kings were,
still are, blessed in his name, not to mention cornerstones,
banners, airplanes, water, and fire. And since 311 *anno
Domini,* when Constantine, the ruler of this world, al-
lowed himself to be baptized, not only the Jews but almost
all minorities have been hounded in his name.

On a beach of the Pacific, in a swimming pool in Rotter-
dam, in churches and chapels, or in the small circle of a
"floating" parish, en masse and singly, in a continuous
stream, people are baptized in his name. He is the God of
European civilization, of Christian culture. When he suits
the context, his name opens and closes political declara-
tions and papal pronouncements. Such a dead, unlikely
piece of public property, as he rolls off the presses! Whoever speaks or writes about him is an accomplice to his
plight.

The chroniclers of his time do not mention him, except
one. His lot was cast in an obscure corner of the world.
He died a shameful death, but not quite the worst. It can
be described rather exactly. He was crucified, on an upright stake with a crossbeam at its top, forming a T.
The hands were nailed to the crossbeam, through the
wristbone. The feet were lashed or nailed to the upright.
Death due to exhaustion; hunger, thirst, mosquitoes, hor-
nets. Due, also, to the eyes of people: bewildered, mocking,
curious, vacant. Two or three days were usually required.
With him things moved rather quickly; it took only a few
hours. The mound where it happened was called Golgotha,
meaning Skull Place. It was something like the rubbish-
dump of a city in Asia today.

He was sentenced to death as a heretic. "He has blas-
phemed God; he opposes the temple," cried the religious

leaders of his country, and, in the same breath, "He is against the Emperor, against the occupying forces, against the established order. He is a dangerous political adventurer." The Roman procurator doesn't take all this too seriously; but he goes along with it, anyhow—every people, now and then, is bent on bread and circuses. And blood.

What a death! By means of an arbitrary and corrupt proceeding, he is gotten rid of, and life goes on. A group of friends and relatives keep his name alive in memory, and pass his story on.

Ten, twenty, thirty years pass by, after his death. All kinds of stories and testimonials concerning him circulate, all with the identical downbeat: *him*. He is it, the unforgettable man. Little anecdotes, rather clumsily related at times, venturesome lyrical contemplations, highly personal memoirs—so arranged and orchestrated that, in those varied fragments of tradition, his unique meaning is preserved.

What comes through to me, when I read those gospel texts and their learned commentaries over and over, when I listen to the Scriptures again and again?

He loves people, obviously; he is always with people, he seeks them out. And they seek him out. Who are they? Army officers, tax collectors, mothers with their children, widows, single women, fishermen, beggars, blind men, money-lenders, people at a party, and scribes. He avoids no one who seeks his company, does not refuse a single human contact, gives up on nobody in advance. He's not particular; he belongs to everybody, is always free for whomever he runs into. He wins people by the open-minded way he walks up to them. And he lets himself be won and disarmed—for example, by that woman from be-

yond the confines of Israel who urges her case so long that
he does what she asks—just a small miracle—the cure of
her little girl.

But he shies away from "publicity," never plays to "his
public." He goes apart, to hidden places, to be alone, to
pray.

In a society rife with factions, sects, subcultures, ranks and
classes, functionaries, bureaucracy, communication gaps,
precise standards of conduct, religious laws, and a perfect
babel of tongues, he moves about like the man who always
knows better than that, who believes that things can be
otherwise.

In a world where one greets only his brothers and knows
only his kinfolk, he breaks out of the shell of the family
circle, which in turn has no idea what he's all about, and
so is against him and has pronounced him mad. And he is
deeply touched, profoundly moved by people, no matter
who they are or what they're like, whether rich or poor.
He is averse to no one, he never considers himself too good
for anybody.

No matter who they are, he approaches them directly and
asks, "Who are you? What are you living for? Why aren't
you living?"

And then he tells them, "You must be born anew, so
must I. It can be yours—that Kingdom of God, that new
start—yours, with all your struggles for prestige, only if
you are willing to become poor, a child; only if you are
willing to recognize yourself in the least of people."

Princes and princesses can find him, too, as can all those
around the world to whom they are related by ties of

blood, rank, or money, intent upon their nocturnal safaris or drawn together in their tents of Persian tapestry—all those poor rich people can find him, too. But to find him, they are certainly going to have to part with their gold, to go and sell everything, to break their pattern of anxiety and heaping up riches, that blind and rapacious way of life —accumulating capital, making profit, managing both the market and public opinion.

He is moved by them, for camels will sooner creep through the eye of a needle than they will give up their position for the sake of the poor. Most of the time, they go sadly away from him, for the sake of their many possessions.

There is, in his whole bearing, not a trace of servility or time-serving. He rejects every dichotomy (undefiled/defiled, we/they) which would make people unfree, belittle them, or lay unbearable burdens upon them. And he is the chattel of no man, no tradition, and no received idea of God. This is the source of the astonishment and scandal which can be sensed on nearly every page of the gospel.

He knew no fear, we might almost say. This despite the fact, as is clear from the oldest testimony, that he was set upon and tried as sorely as any one of us.

With unprecedented effect, he faced the human chaos, the frenzy, the storms, the shrieking of the possessed. He could handle them, demons and all, obviously. Including the powers-that-be. He didn't believe that they were *unquestionably right*, that they were *the last word*. He saw, he said, satan falling from the heavens, the god of the established order dethroned. He could exorcize devils (who still believes in them?); he challenged the gods, for example, when he defined the accusers of the adulterous woman with the words, "Whoever is without sin, throw the first stone at her"—and they drifted off, the oldest first.

By doing, by doing things like this—far from being naive or credulous (he knows what's going on in people)—he stood up like a brother, a fellow-victim, for all those who are poor, for the pitiful, the innocuous, in brief, for us. Just as we are, living out the drudgery of our small lives around the lake of Galilee ("at that time"), he accepts us; and he speaks to us, pays attention to us, and has compassion for our weakest point, for what has gone awry in every one of us.

What does he say to us? The most ordinary things. He talks about the having of children, and about planting crops and how you must wait with good trust and not too much fuss for them to come up. He talks about the smallest seed, how it becomes a tree, and how this is the way God works, and how it works with his kingdom in this world. What an optimist!

Many words, wise sayings, proverbs and discourses are attributed to him in the gospels. A good deal of it was, in fact, placed on his lips, in the course of time, by his followers—as followers have ever been wont to do. But it is surely his very own voice we hear where we read: Do not be anxious for your life, for your body, for eating and drinking, for tomorrow.

What kind of philosophy of life is that? What am I supposed to do with it? It is not a philosophy of life, not a handbook for daily use nor a general operating principle. It is as useless as a prophecy; it is a vision that will never develop into an economic system. But it is, perhaps, a summons so to live that something begins to dawn on me, a kind of suspicion: *Blest are the poor in spirit.*

He speaks with obvious and unprecedented authority. He says, "In the beginning was not what we are now—mutually unfaithful and vengeful—in the beginning was compassion, the simple idea that you just don't give the other person stones for bread. The original idea is friendship.

"In the beginning that is what was pondered, dreamt about, willed, and set in motion. That is the vision we have all been woven of, and to which we are all called," he says. *"In the beginning* is our future."

The people say, mockingly, "It would almost seem as though you were there, in person, actually present, in the beginning—and you're not even fifty years old!"

Did he bring something new? He was a Jew, and in the synagogue of Nazareth he listened to and learned the creed of Israel: parables, rules of life, psalms and prophecies, visions of justice. He was one of the people in the long line which, "at that time," sought baptism from the ascetic, monkish man, named John, on the bank of the Jordan, because they were conscious of their guilt, and were longing for a turnabout-conversion, and for a new beginning.

He sought that new beginning in the tradition of his own people: in the books of Moses and the prophets. In the Law. But "law" is an inadequate and confusing translation of the Hebrew word *tōrāh*, which means: inspiriting teaching, liberating wisdom; well of inspiration, where the purest streams of Israel's life-experience have joined.

The words-of-the-law present: insight into the human heart, so erratic and contradictory; detailed guidance for daily conduct, so that human-being (everything which, in the name of God, binds/obligates people to each other) is safeguarded and continues to be acknowledged in its full range and mettle. The teachings of the Law are intended to engender fidelity to the original idea: justice. The wisdom of the Law aims at making the vision an experience: Man created to be friend-and-friend, word and response, I and you.

"Limpid water," "heart-refreshing," "nothing but peace," "more precious than pure gold"—these are the names for the-words-of-the-law.

Since the days of Israel's darkening and exile, when the vision seemed belied for good, when there was no crown and no temple any more, that jungle which the world at bottom is, was sung—as man-at-the-starting-line, a child who is in the beginning; someone more creative than the existing world, more original than the fate which rules us, more lasting than the chaos, than the ghetto into which we are dumped. As it is written:

> The Lord begot me, the firstborn of his ways,
> the forerunner of his prodigies of long ago. . . .
> When there were no depths I was brought forth,
> when there were no fountains or springs of water. . . .
> When he made firm the skies above. . . .
> When he set for the sea its limit. . . .
> then I was his delight day by day,
> playing before him all the while. . . .
> and I find delight in the children of men.*

This is the wisdom he has imbibed and revered, this the tutelage by which he has been raised. This is the vision he has beheld and voiced.

He brought nothing new. To this day, he who has been called "the way" by his followers, is, first of all, the way *back* to the writings of Israel. So that we, like trees near a spring, would stand rooted in the conscience of Israel, summoned to make a world worthy of a human being, for everybody. Like all the prophets who preceded him, he is the mediator between "in the beginning" and "now."

But when, "at that time," moving about in his native region of Galilee, he noticed that the first flowering of the Torah had withered, overgrown by arbitrarily prescribed pious practices, and gradually choked off by interpretations derived from ephemeral and even competing interests; and when he could not but learn, by hard experience, how the inspiriting teaching of the Law had degenerated in the mouths of priests, lawyers, and theologians into soul-killing hair-splitting and letter-worshipping, at the expense of the poor and the unemancipated (those people who don't know the Law), and thus was no longer a source of strength but another form of oppression—

then he dared, like a prophet, a called-one, to criticize the current formulations and interpretations of his own religious and moral tradition. And he did not hesitate, on his own responsibility, to set aside the so-called sacred Law and force of custom.

When he went to the synagogue on the sabbath one time, he met a man who had a withered hand. All those present watched him carefully, to see whether he would undertake the cure of that man on the sabbath—so that they might accuse him of not observing the Law.

He said to the man with the withered hand: Come and stand here, in the center. Then he posed this question to them: "Which is better, to do a good deed, on the sabbath day, or to do evil? To save someone on the sabbath, or to let someone be lost?"

Every one of them kept his mouth shut.

Angry, he looked round at the circle, grieved by their

hardness of heart. Then he said to the man in the middle: Put your hand out. He put his hand out—and was cured.

To people who hold the Law in their hands and, appealing to Moses, are bent on condemning, expelling, and stoning each other, he says, "Because your hearts were hardened, this is how you have understood and acted; but in the beginning it was not so." And like all the prophets who preceded him, but with a style and grace all his own, he dared to interpret anew the deepest intention, the key-words and ideas of the Law. He himself calls this *fulfilling* the Law, as in the parable of man-and-his-neighbor, of man fallen into the hands of men, of the Good Samaritan.

In this parable, that whole sacred philosophy of life and venerable wisdom which is called the Law is expressed and assessed anew. Israel's original vision of a world worthy of a human being is realized (says this deceptively simple story) wherever a single man no longer runs away, but says No, and looks at the other, picks him up, and pays for him —wherever a single man lets himself be persuaded by the defenselessness of the other.

This parable of the-helper-and-the-helped is the story of one who recognizes himself in the other: He is like me; I am like him, every bit as expendable and assailable, just as easily laid low and robbed. The Samaritan recognizes himself in that beaten dog by the wayside because he is a beaten dog himself, a stranger in Israel, without any rights, one who is really not even supposed to be there.

A man recognizes himself in another man when he himself has become nothing more (or less) than a man. (Hence, the gluttons, the big spenders, the gods cannot help, can only hurt each other; hence, the dividers of the world move among themselves like the *blind leading the blind,* and eat each other up.) The recognition of oneself in another is purified experience of life. And purified life-experience is another word for "conscience."

To do justice is to do or act according to this conscience, to do unto others as you would have others do unto you. No more. But it is immeasurably more than being nice, or even what people usually call love. It is more than anything you are able to feel. But you are able to discern it. And choose it.

The most radical formulation of this call to justice—which in good Christian usage is known as the Commandment "love thy neighbor"—is "love thy enemy." The Samaritan of the parable was, "at that time," the enemy of the upright Jew who was heading home to Jericho from Jerusalem, convinced that he was one of the true worshippers of God, and that the Samaritans were only religious mongrels. But what does it tell you? To love your enemy, your hangman, the one who walks all over you, exploits you. Out of purified life-experience, to recognize the other, who is your opponent, as your fellow-victim. I am like him, he is like me; somewhere we are known and willed as people-for-one-another, our source is one and the same vision—and when that vision is darkened in any single one of us, the light of life is diminished in all.

"To love" means, in the language of that impossible messianic maxim, to know another in the very source of his being; to bid him return there, seeing how alienated he is from it; to appeal to the vision which is dying in him; to say, "you, brother"; to respond to him and to look him full in the face, as though you were God. To be God for him, to be the voice of his conscience. Only he who knows from his own purified life-experience that he himself is untrustworthy—in the twinking of an eye, a snap of the fingers, the very opposite of the man he should be, a beast and no longer a man—only he who, even then, believes that a new beginning is still possible for him, only such a man can stand up to his enemy, can resist him yet keep faith with him, can love him as himself.

Did he bring anything new? He says, "You were talking about God? I tell you, God loves his enemies, and through my mouth he says to you: Love your enemy." ("Be perfect, as your Father in heaven is perfect.") God says, "It is not a question of me—what matters is that other man who draws near to you, your neighbor, your enemy."

God points away from himself, toward every human being. God himself is that least of the brethren, that beaten dog by the wayside. God is merciful—he knows from experience what it is to be a stranger, a wet-back, in this world.

Did he bring anything new? He pointed the way back to a God who does not stand upon his rights nor exact his due, merciless and unapproachable, who is not persuaded by bloody sacrifices and similar performances. Rather, in the beginning, and ever after, he is neighbor to all that lives, shepherd of the lost ewe lamb. And, as David for Absalom, he cries out for every son of man who is estranged from his source, and lost.

He did not bring anything "new." But the power that went out from his words was so shattering, went so far beyond the prevailing Jewish teaching and worship, that he was branded a heretic and done away with as a blasphemer. Some people recognized in him the unadulterated sound of the voice of the God of Israel. They said, "In this man there lives once more the name of God. This is he who was to come; now we need no longer await another, because in him the purpose of the Law has been realized, has been summed up. Here, in the flesh, is the word who unveils the original vision of our tradition; who makes straight, once more, the way of Israel's words. True, there have been others, also, prophetic teachers who had this kind of power, but as far as we are concerned (his followers say) it was he in whom the Voice spoke to us, he who said to us: *I make all things new."*

One of those followers is an ardent young Jew, perhaps twenty years old, dubbed "son of thunder." He is seer, poet, and thinker. An eagle who peers into the sun. A good sixty years after his relatively short but intense friendship with Jesus of Nazareth, an aged angel now, smitten by years, confined to an island and destined for the boiling oil, he witnesses: "He has made all things new. . . . I, John, have heard and seen." Of all the eyewitness followers, he is the most consistent, apodictic, demanding. For to him is attributed the most profound and soaring account of the first hundred years of the Jesus movement: the so-called Fourth Gospel, with its prologue, that song of word-and-flesh—happily a song and not a binding definition; a poem not a dogma.

John says: He is the word from in-the-beginning, from before-the-primordial-waters, the void, this uninhabitable world. From him, out of him, were all things in this world, in myself, put in order, made meaningful. From him, out of him, through him, am I who I am. All things are darkness, compared with him. He is the real light. We are strange; he is friend. He alone is our guide. The Lord begot him, the firstborn of his ways,/ the forerunner of his prodigies of long ago./ When there were no depths he was brought forth.*

In the beginning was he the word. Then he was his delight day by day. In the beginning, already, was he—turned toward our God.

That word became flesh, John says. Flesh is, for John, what everyone is: transitory, palpably there. Flesh is accidental form, a beautiful-ugly face, to be material, to be there, here and there, fleeting, grass.

I-shall-be-there-for-you, that is Israel's word for God. I shall be there for you in-the-flesh, says this song. As tangible and real as one human being can ever be for another. I shall be there.

He who would hear, see, and touch God, says this song, must go into this world of people. Nowhere else does God come to light, except in people who are tangible, negligible, and exposed.

We—not I alone, God knows how prone I am to private visions, says John—we, a group of us, all eyewitnesses, have touched him with our hands, have seen how magnificent he is. We have seen the irrefutable authority, the sheer weight of that word. And we experienced his power when he washed our feet, like a slave, like the least among us; when he was murdered like a slave, his flesh scorched like grass. Then we could find no words except, "My Lord and my God."

Other followers have handed down their own accounts of what he (*he,* their common refrain) meant to them. They are more restrained, their language less powerful, less unbending and uncompromising, often differently nuanced, and they often draw upon traditions different from John's. But always, from the depths of their unique shared experience, they proclaim how profoundly he touched their lives.

Deaf and dumb, he opened me to the Voice. He said: Be open, and I was open. He raised the dead, going beyond even that last limit. He broke through the laws of nature, gravity, the closed circuit, the treadmill of existence: he walked upon the water.

Stories of miracles, figures of speech, parables; apparently the only language suited to their subject and capable of expressing their amazement and deep emotion about him; efforts not to fail altogether in trying to do justice to the power that went out from him.

In the light cast by his life, his death has been interpreted as that ultimate (and original) moment in which his meaning becomes visible. And the power which, "in the days of his mortal life," went out from him, is fathomed, and is named: *God's* power. They went on to say: He was the Son of God, he has died for us. He has redeemed us. He has shed his blood unto the forgiveness of sin.

In all the oldest documents of Christian tradition, one senses a groping for such formulations as may preserve his memory. They approach his life from many different angles, in different keys, recording testimonials which overlap, vary, complete and correct each other with a freedom we are not likely to comprehend very readily. They contain no systematic theology, as yet, nor any one formula which has wholly captured him; nor any exclusive view of him which is rammed through at the expense of other views and intuitions. That happens only later, when his followers—cut off from their original Jewish context—no longer catch the biblical overtones and undertones of the very language they are using. It is then that their words become unintelligible terms, shouted with a raspy voice; an exclusive idiom safeguarding essential definitions and philosophical conclusions which rob you, at the very outset, of the chance and desire to think the matter over yourself.

Or those rich tones from Israel are drowned out by ecclesiastical jargon: "He has redeemed us on the cross, by his blood"—words which today evoke memories that are like bad dreams, provoke angry outbursts, and perpetuate old misapprehensions; a "dogma," no less, which, in a manner eliciting no corresponding feeling in the indicted, declares everybody guilty of his death and disparages them all (they all understand it wrongly, of course—it was explained to them wrongly, of course); conversation-stoppers, which order every true Christian to feel redeemed and happy. "In what sense has the death of Christ redeemed us, when, in fact, nobody feels redeemed?" Jung asks. The only thing which many people, after the long, confused period of their youth, are able to do with words like "redeemed" is to try to forget them, to write off that whole lingo as irrelevant, revealing nothing.

Would it still be possible, ever, to bring those words, "cross," "redemption," "blood," back from their exile, and to understand them anew, as full of promise and liberation as they were originally meant to be?

He died for us. He lived for people. He drank the cup we must drink. He has made himself the advocate and proxy of the poor. He has seen through their situation, how they are victimized, and he has made their burdens and interests his own. And for that, the dividers of the world have repaid him. That life he chose cost him his life.

He has redeemed us. We were big people, overweight, wise, with all our might—"each other's underlings, imprisoned in our dreaming"; enslaved, for example, by the illusion that there is simply no place to begin, that you can't fight City Hall; that it all comes down to "choose your own poison." You can join in with the keeners, or sigh resignedly, or sit the whole business out in dead silence, according to your temperament. You were born that way, and you can't get born anew. And so forth and so on. . . . *But,*

he set me on fire with the insight that I could begin anew —I saw in him that it could be done, because he began anew with everyone.

When I was below zero (below *me*), shivering with disillusionment, he approached and spoke to me, put the choice squarely before me: Do you want to stay dead, or do you want to come alive? He took me as he found me, did not accuse me of my past, but asked me: Do you want to go on like this, or do you want a change? Do you identify with what lies behind you, in which case you are not fit for the kingdom of God, or do you identify with the future?

But then, is there a future? I asked.

Come with me, he answered.

He released the potential for growth which had nearly died in me. He infused new life into me, when I was bloodless and soulless, confused and confusing, as people are who can no longer believe that their paltry lives shall yet be justified and find their answer, and who no longer have any hope for the future. It was as though he had sprinkled me with his own lifeblood, his own soul, vitality, much as people were sprinkled with blood in Israel's traditional liturgy, as a sign that their God wanted to scatter the seed of his soul-power, his spirit, all over them.

It was as though, through him, I had been bound anew to others, to all the potentialities with which people are endowed. As though he had donated his blood to me, was my donor—and thus I was received anew into the fellowship of the living: "a new covenant in his blood."

The soul-power that went out from him to me was stronger, more evident, than the powerlessness I experience in myself. The new life which he stirs up in me is more truly *me* than all my failings; his light is stronger than the darkness in me; his faithfulness is greater than my bad faith, or anybody's: "His blood is the forgiveness of my sins." And it is not me alone he has redeemed. "He has shed his blood for us all."

They dragged him to Golgotha, the Place of the Skull. After they crucified him, they divided up his garments and cast lots for his tunic. It was, perhaps, nine o'clock in the morning, when they crucified him, together with a pair of robbers, one at his left hand, the other at his right. People passing by scoffed at him, and the priests and the scribes sneered among themselves, "He has saved others; himself he cannot save."

Now it was noon, and darkness fell over all the land. Then it was three o'clock in the afternoon. Then he cried: *Eli, Eli, lema sabachtani?* that is, My God, my God, why hast thou forsaken me? Then he cried out something unintelligible, and was dead.

When the Roman officer who was standing near him, keeping an eye on him, saw that he had given up the ghost, and the way he had died, he cried out: This is the son of God.

That he, crucified as a slave—who still knows what slaves are, seeing that slavery was abolished in 1863?—that he is still not lost for good (he is risen) means: he is known, saved, by God. It means that God saves the least of people. You must become the least, in order that this God of Jesus can be your God and father.

"His cross is the sign of our salvation" means the least

of human lives, the most miserable lot, is not meaningless, going nowhere, without a future; is not fatherless.

"He is the son of God." In the language of the bible that means he was filled with the power of God; he acted in the spirit of God; was, by his choice of all who are deprived of justice, a kindred spirit of God; image and likeness of the God of the poor. Called by God; born of God.

By reason of this very faith-experience he was called the Messiah, Christ. The one sent in the name of God, in whose life of dismal failure some people recognized God's power. Messiah, a name for "the established chaos" turned upside-down; first-born of another order; born of God. The last who became the first.

"Man" was one of his titles. Man as intended in the beginning. The son of Man.

For those who have loved his appearance in the flesh and have not turned their eyes away from his marred figure, he has become the vision of man with a future, indestructibly, infectiously man. In him they have recognized themselves: what they must do, what awaits them.

He is called God. The more his followers spread out from their own country and from the sources of their own tradition, the more eager are they, contrary to Jewish usage, to call him by that name which is no name.

More and more he is "adored." And less and less, imitated. He is "not of this world"; how should we, then, be able to do what he has done? Besides (we say), he has done it already, for us, in place of us. And once that little word "God" has become the vaguest of all epithets for what is highest and deepest in the soul and the universe, he becomes the vaguest man of all, the "God-man," and it's all over; we may as well believe in him. He turns into a dream-figure, a wish-fulfilment, a projection of our better selves. A mythical, prehistoric figure, as occurs in all religions. He becomes a tale too beautiful to be true: the Divine Savior, the Most Holy Redeemer, our Lord'n Savyer Jeezis Christ.

His name was Jesus, Jeshua; or else, Jeshu, in his native tongue. He was named after Joshua, the successor of Moses, who led the twelve tribes of Israel into the promised land. A popular name; Israel swarmed in those days with kids called Jesus. "Of Nazareth," a kind of surname. Not "of Jerusalem," that center of law and tradition, liturgy and national dreams. He hails from a hamlet from which, in the parlance of the people of his day, no good could come.

He still bears the name of people and of a patch of Jewish land. He shared the time and lot of poor fishermen and farmers. He is, still, a sorry-looking beginning, in every hick-town in the world.

❧ IN THE BEGINNING

In the beginning
was the word
and the word was
in the presence
of our God
and the word itself
was God—
in the beginning
already

was the word
turned
toward our God.

All things
are
through the word,
apart from him
not a thing became,
nothing of all
the things which are.

In the word
was life
and the life was
the light
for mankind.
And the light shines
in darkness
and the darkness
did not overwhelm
the light.

The word
the one true light
enlightening every one
who comes into this world,
he was in this world—
the world became
through the word.
Yet the world
was unwilling
to know the word.

He came into his house.
His own have not received him.

But all who did
receive him,
he has enabled them
to do
what is undoable:
to become
children of God,
all who
entrust themselves
to his name
who dare to do so.
Not from flesh and blood
with might and main
not by their own strength
have they been born
but of God.

The word
has become flesh
has pitched his tent
in our midst.
We ourselves
have seen his light—
it weighs us down
it lifts us up
shines through us—
at last we found
no words but these:
he is
the father's own
and only son,

is friendship
and truth.

Out of his fullness
all of us
have received
abounding grace.

The words of the law
were given through Moses.
Friendship, grace
unfailing faithfulness
have come to us
through Jesus Messiah.

No one has ever
seen God.
The true son,
only son, God,
whose nature it is
to be in the bosom
of the father

he alone
is
our guide.

*The Prologue of St. John's gospel
translated anew, freely.*

❧ THREE LITTLE WORDS

What did he look like? Did he have an open face? Was
he tall or short? Was he witty, shy? Difficult, or easy to

deal with? Was he warm-blooded and spontaneous, or in-
hibited? Did he seem frustrated? Was he talented? Was he
married? Who were his teachers? What were things like at
home? Were they an average-sized Jewish family? Poor?
What kind of man was his father? What did he do all
those years before he began his public life?

To none of these questions, nor to many others, do we have
a definite answer. The four gospels which, as written documents, are unlike any other historical or literary writings,
make at best only a casual effort at a continuous narrative,
and they provide neither his life-story nor a psychological
profile. Nor were they ever intended to do so. Scarcely a
single date has come down to us, and our modern western
craving for precise data and careful delineation must go
quite unsatisfied.

Twenty-five years after his death, when word of him and
his first followers and the glad tidings are collected in the
oldest of the gospels, that of Mark, it does not prove a book
replete with powerful examples, pious details, or droll
flourishes—the kind of interest, quite understandable,
which turns out sometimes rather moving, but generally
cheap or bizarre apocrypha.

Mark's gospel is a testimonial of faith, put together from
brief, or sometimes extended stories, each in turn going
back again to the beginning, and all striving to say just this
one thing: He is *it*. That it is he who says to me: Be not
anxious for your life; pray in secret; when someone strikes
you, do not strike back; follow me. He, he says these
things. That I must forgive seventy times seven, that I
must clothe the naked (not because that is nice and human, but because they are naked). He it is who says to me:

I may be a living dead man and a hearing deaf man; the lame walk, and the prisoners are set free.

In each of its little stories, this gospel testifies anew that "he is it." Is what? The Messiah, the one who is to come. But what does that mean? That he serves, functions, as the promise of ·justice on earth *some*time; that he vividly evokes that future for us and keeps alive in us the hope that, by God, it is possible.

He is it. What? The Son of God. That means God permits himself to be known in him as breathing-space and faithfulness and patience, as the one whom all earthly fatherhood must mirror.

He is the revelation of God, says the gospel. He is the sign, the promise, the pledged word that the God of Israel has thrown his arms wide to everyone. Jesus is God-at-his-clearest, as clear as man-is-for-others, as clear as "love one another."

He—dead, buried, and withdrawn by God from the doom and power of death—he is it, says the gospel. In him the meaning of your existence comes to light: that the God whom he calls his Father turns himself toward you, that he is à God of people, of the living. And Jesus, what is his meaning? He "means" God saves, God is love.

He is man's revelation-in-the-making, the promise-in-the-flesh, he *is* the sign—the sign that every human being can open up to God, can turn toward, convert to God. At last, a man who is open, the gospel attests of him. He is it, at last, bone of our bone and flesh of our flesh. He is man-at-his-clearest: abundant light; there is nothing behind or beyond "love one another." He has fulfilled those words.

The gospel says he is the most transparent, unambiguous, and human-relations-expert word about man. Image and likeness of man. He is the least veiled, least obscure word about God. He who sees him, sees the father. He is the living parable of God.

He is the most radical summons to justice conceivable —but the oldest evidence nowhere suggests that he would be the only such radical summons to justice; at his side, before and after him, there is room for every prophet, for every Francis of Assisi, every Amos, yes, for every Marx and Martin Luther King. He is, together with all those others, the parable of the Kingdom of God. He is the image and likeness of every man and his neighbor. In him is made manifest all those people who have ever gone, and who are still to go, "where no roads go, go everywhere." In him can be heard the voice who cries "where is your brother?" He bears, he carries on, the name of the God of the poor; he is called the Lord.

What he was, above all, has been handed down in the gospel: spirit who gives life. In that light, everything that was transitory about him, all that was bound up with time and language, faded away; details and incidentals, like flesh and hay and grass, went up in smoke.

He is departed, dead, and none can go where he is, says the gospel. You can't bump into him any more, and ask questions. He doesn't solve anything for you; he can't spare you from anything, not a single responsibility. You can't use him for a god, a culture, a church, a high official, a sacrament. He is useless to us, except for those three little words, referring us right back to each other: love one another.

In those words his meaning opens up to us. If we *do* them. In a gesture, one to the other—bread broken and shared—he can appear to us. In people who do that, you can see him.

Any resemblance to living persons is not only not excluded but explicitly intended, hoped for. By so doing, every one can be like him, substantially.

Images and words from Israel's whole tradition of belief become names for him, in the gospel. As they become names for every one who chooses life as he did.

The gospel brings me this message from him: I am the light; you are the light.

❧ TWENTY-NINE NAMES FOR JESUS OF NAZARETH

neighbor   friend   Jew   seed
tree-by-the-spring   bridegroom   way

a-dream-of-a-man   open-door   cornerstone
key   lion-of-judah   lamb   a-just-man

shepherd   pearl   blossoming-bud   fish   bread
word   vine   son-of   God   servant

living-water   morning-star   front-runner
one-and-only   name-on-the-tip-of-the-tongue-forever

❧ OF BREAKING AND SHARING

He who is ready to give what he has, he shall live. Wherever people realize this and do it, says Christianity (and sings it, too, in strains both hard and sweet), there *presto* is that peace which surpasseth understanding. And the love of God our Father. And the fellowship of the Holy Spirit.

There does the Kingdom of God draw near. There the Body is built up. Body of Christ.

Quite a barrage of capital letters and big words. Is there no simpler way to say it? Hardly.

Even though they mean, after all, the simplest thing in the world. Like what?

The common ordinary thrilling fact that people trust each other; accept a piece of bread from someone else's hand; extend credit to each other; like, admire, love each other; or don't, and still don't bite each other, tear each other apart, or just let each other go hang. But are there really people like that? Yes, there really are, says the gospel, there are people like that: one body of people, each for the other, no one out for himself.

Paul, one of the most smitten of the Jesus people from that day to this, even claims to believe that this union of I-you-he is stronger and older than death. It is a body *opposed* to death. To be part of that union is to rise from the dead, to live through and beyond death. He who does not have part in it, doesn't believe in it, and thinks it's impossible—that person, says Paul, has no idea of God.

There has come down from of old a kind of people's play, in which that union of mutual trust is celebrated. A perfectly simple, almost naive gesture of hope, self-knowledge, human understanding, and courage to live: breaking and sharing bread with each other, and with that, singing a song.

In Christian tradition, that play is called "the eucharist." Again, such a difficult word.

Eucharist: a rite, a play for people who have recognized in Jesus of Nazareth the follower, the descendant of God, the front-runner in a long string of pathfinders, the corner-stone of the City of Peace.

They came together "in one or another house" * with joy in their hearts, say the oldest records of that movement which was called (deprecatingly) "the Way." ** And why did they assemble? To break bread together: picture of a way of life which dares to be unpretentious. Just too elementary to be some scholarly acquired-behavior-pattern.

Whoever doesn't really believe in it, in that pulsing conglomerate of people; whoever says: I just can't do it, it's too much for me—he had better stay out of it. You can't celebrate your dividedness, your unbelief. But you can celebrate your desire for wholeness, yes, and your trying to believe. Whoever would have it so: I am your bread, you my bread, and he is our bread—such a person, no matter who, can join in.

But those who do gather, even till today, "in one or another house" to celebrate the eucharist may have to take account of what Paul wrote to "the Way" in his first Epistle** to the church at Corinth, sometime between 50 and 70 A.D.—

"As long as I am writing, I do want to tell you that your religious gatherings are conducted in a way which does you perhaps more harm than good. I hear that discord reigns when you gather in your church, and I believe it, too, at least in part. Because it needs must be that dissensions arise among you, if it is to become clear who among you is trustworthy.

"The way you are presently conducting your gatherings, there can be no question of a genuine Lord's Supper, since all are so intent upon gobbling up their own stores that some go hungry and others get drunk. After all, you have

houses to eat and drink in. Or do you despise the intention* of God, and will you not break and share your bread
with those who have nothing?

"I myself have received from the Lord what in turn I
have handed down to you: that the Lord Jesus, on the
night in which he was betrayed, took bread and said, 'This
is my body for you; do this in memory of me.' In the same
way, he took the cup, saying, 'This cup is the new covenant in my blood. Whenever you drink of it, do it in
memory of me.'

"Whenever you eat this bread and drink this cup, you
proclaim, until he comes, that our Lord has given himself,
even unto death."

YOU WHO KNOW

You who know what goes on in people,
the hoping, doubting
dullness, passion, pleasure, wavering

You who discern our thoughts
and measure all our words by truth
and grasp at once the things
we cannot put in words

You try our hearts
and you are larger than our hearts,
you keep an eye on every one of us

and no one ever lacks a name with you
and no one falls but he falls in your hands
and no one lives but his life moves toward you.

But no one has ever seen your face.
In all this world you are inaudible,

your voice does not echo
deep in the earth, nor from the heights of heaven.

And no one who has entered death's domain
ever has returned
to bring us back your greetings.
With tender ties to you, we bear your name.
You alone know what that betokens,
not we.

We journey through the world with eyes unopen.
But sometimes we ourselves recall a name,
an ancient story we were handed down,
touching a man who trembled with your power,
Jesus of Nazareth, a Jewish man.

In him your grace was said to be transparent
your gentle, constant ways.
In him, we were told,
once for all there came to light
what you are really like:
the selfless, defenseless
servant of people.

He was the way we all would want to be:
a man of God, a friend,
a light, a shepherd,
one who did not live to look out for himself,
and did not go to death in vain and fruitless.

One who on his final night
among the living
took the bread and passed it all around,
and said these words:
take, eat, this is my body—
thus should you do to keep my memory.

Then raising high the cup, he spoke the words:
this is the new covenant, this is my blood,
and I shall shed it
that your sins may be forgiven.
Whenever you shall drink this cup,
think then of me.

To keep his memory
therefore, now we take
this bread; we break it, too,
for each other,
that we may realize
what lies ahead for us
if we choose to
follow after.

As you have saved
your son from death,
O God, as he
died and was buried,
yet lives with you:

then save us, too,
sustain us in living,
pull us, too,
through our dying
now.

And make us new;
for why save him
and not us?

we are likewise
human.

❧ THEN IT WAS

Then it was, O living God,
you changed my sadness into joy.
Then you cried out: *be man*
and stones were no more silent,
we were born—
you made us human beings
one by one.
Then you gave your name:
I shall be there
I shall be there like bread
close as a friend
like a word.

Then you called one from many
and you asked
if he wanted to be light
of your light,
if he wanted to be human
as you intended man to be.
Him we celebrate and sing and call to mind,
Jesus of Nazareth.

When his hour had come
when he was in great fear
he cried aloud to you above
and looked around
on every side,
and found no one to help him.

Then drawing on the spirit
deep in him
he stayed upright to the end,
and recklessly, not thinking twice
he did a very ordinary thing
for a man
who is
indestructibly man:

he gave himself
like a voice that seeks an echo
like someone sharing bread
with someone else
while saying, even wordlessly:
this is my body—
much as a man
who lets his cup go round
might say: Here I am,
won't you drink of me?

His name and what he did
we call to mind,
to be some day who he was:
your son—
to be some day where he is:
with you.

That is why we take
this bread, this cup
and look for one another
to be human.

❧ SAVE US—FROM US

God and father
source of life
voice and heart
our maker
you—or was it not
you who made us
to look out for and support each other?
Who else can save us from ourselves
if not your power in us, your word in us?
Be restless in us
be clear light in us
be insight in us, knowledge, tireless patience.
Be thirst in us which nothing can allay
for justice and for peace.

To you we pray: against ourselves
against preferring not to know
against the silent majority in us
against the slyness of our economic politics
against the double-talk, the half-truths,
the whole lies,
against the trade in arms,
against the death of thousands, every day—
how long has it not gone on—
against napalm and scorched earth,
against the putting down of all the blacks
in Surinam, Angola, here in Holland
in South America, in North America
exploited by our affluence
abhorred and feared for being

as you created them—
all things you willed to make
you wanted to be good and very good,
why do all things go the way they go,
why do we do the things we do?

Are you mighty? Then free them
from our hands.
Have you no might? Then you are one of those
foredoomed to death, yet never having lived.
Are you the God who said:
"I shall be there for you"?
Then be God for our neighbors far away,
your people, all the world,
not people, worms like him
they kicked and sold and crucified,
Jesus your son.

We pray to you, for all those people
who have to live with violence,
who hardly can expect
the future will bring anything
but more disasters on their heads;

for all who tire of talking peace
of struggling for justice,
who no longer believe it can change,
for those worn down and sceptical
not up to any more resistance.

We pray to you, for those who don't give up,
for freedom-fighters and guerillas:
that they stay at their posts, alert and unflinching;
that we may never be without

people who can stand against
incomprehension and betrayal.

For ourselves, who have bread and money
and more than that:
that we may realize in what ways
we help maintain this chaos,
and how we are engaged
in the business of war.

For all who live in affluence
yet have no hope, no life that is fulfilling,
who are damaged in their depths,
divided and grown lonely,
imprisoned by their power and their possessions.

Thus we come to you,
our mouth full of words, our heart heavy,
we, accused by the voice of our conscience
which declares that this cannot go on—

we people, known and called by you,
responsible, bound to respond,
we people, like that one from our ranks
who is named—long ago and hoping for the best—
your son, the firstborn of the dead,
at last—a man, Jesus of Nazareth,

who lived
all that a man is sure to live
whenever he wants to be good,
all that is inhuman and senseless
and insufferable,

who knew hunger, thirst, and loneliness
who was betrayed
who still clung fast to you,
believing: Jesus of Nazareth,

who on the night of his suffering and death
took bread, saying,
"I want to be your food,
I want to share what I am
with you, my neighbor, and with every man,"

who poured a cup of wine
and passed it round, and said:
"I want to be your drink,
I would give my blood and soul
for a new covenant with all people—

"whoever hears me, and turns round, and holds on, does
        good.
He who does good meets God." *

And so we take this bread,
break and share it with each other
in token that we believe
the impossible is possible:
a new covenant in our midst,
justice done, God in our midst.

And so we pass the cup, one to another
in the name of him who said:
Can you drink the cup which I must drink?

❧ WHOEVER CLAIMS THAT GOD

Whoever claims that God
   (which God? My God? The Lord Our God?
   The God of gods? Dear God?)
whoever claims that he is the God, the brother
the fellow-victim of poor people—
he had better realize what he is saying,
for he is saying:
God has no rights and is poor,
exploited, and gagged
like all poor people.

And poor people aren't like us,
they whine and snap
like beaten dogs.
We eat and drink: bread and wine,
and leave our crumbs for the dogs.

Whoever says
I believe in God, I believe in God,
and cries: Lord, Lord,
but must prosper, at any cost,
and makes money
from the daily death-struggle of the poor:
he denies him who said:
I am the God of the poor.

Whoever is comfortable
in the game where money-is-might
and the poor are unfailingly trumped,

whoever thinks: it's not my concern—
what can I do about that?—
and steeped in invincible innocence
washes his hands,
he has hardened his heart
denying the God who has said:
I myself am the poor,
the nameless sacrifice
on the tables of the wealthy countries.

Whoever here and now
extends his hand
takes bread and eats,
by that he says
that he desires a different world
where bread and freedom are
for everyone.
And he who drinks this cup
chooses a new covenant
with all the people.

For all who venture that
things will go for them
the way they went for Jesus
and for God,
the way they go
for all the poor.

You, Jesus Christ
image of God,
image and likeness of man,
you,
yourself the least of men,

your word it is I speak
your bread I eat

is it your death I die?

must I, like you
become
the poorest of the poor?

❧ LINES FOR MY SON
invisibly engraved on his birthstone
(as it is writen: whoever perseveres,
to him a white stone shall be given
whereon is engraved a new name
known by no one but him who receives it.*)

HE WHO WILL NOT
GIVE HIS LIFE,
WILL NOT SHARE
WITH MANY OTHERS
OR ANOTHER,
IS FORLORN.
HE WHO GIVES
WHAT HE HAS,
HE SHALL LIVE
EATEN UP,
HE SHALL KNOW
HE IS BORN.

⮽ IN THE NAME OF JESUS
*(letter to someone who has asked
to be baptized)*

February 18, 1972/Amsterdam
When we gather for your baptism, I'll try to say too little, rather than too much, hoping that all those present will understand without a lot of words.

A variety of people and things will be assembled there, that evening.

People who know each other well, or just a little, or only by sight, or not even that—and yet are still not strangers, because they share the self-same inspiration.

People who take their stand with a tradition called, in a phrase freighted with history, the Christian Faith, and who are quite determined about it, too.

That tradition is age-old and world-wide, and sometimes, whether inside or outside of whatever church, a power goes forth from it which is simply contagious, liberating, healing. There will be people present that evening who try, in one way or another, to participate, to keep pace with the sweep of that power.

Some *things* will be there, too. A book, open. The book of Israel. Because we know where our tradition begins, and what a distance the words have come which nourish our inspiration. The book lies open at the place in Deuteronomy where it is written: "I have set before you life and death, the blessing and the curse. Choose life, then, that you and your descendants may live." *

And because there stood, in the most sacred place in Israel, a seven-branched candlestick, a candlestick with seven candles will stand there that evening, will stand for all the imaginable and unimaginable flames and flickers of light, and the burning desires in all of us.

Light will glow there. Because we believe that we are not blindly and fatally given over to the workings of injustice, guilt, and chaos, but called, known by name, and responsible for each other. And because we believe that the darkness has still not overwhelmed the light.

Still more things. Flowers—you can hardly call them things—not in blossom. Musical instruments, to help raise our piping, quavery, swelling voices. Wine and wine glasses, to encourage us to imbibe a bit of each other as the evening proceeds, and—who knows?—perhaps to drink to friendship. And a jug of water, to pour out. Just as life itself, happiness and sorrow, and the unknown future have been poured out upon us.

And, not least, you: someone who has asked to be baptized. From a depth hidden to all others, you have cried out. And you have learned, slowly and ploddingly, through many years, what it means to ask. And not to know, not to possess. To have nothing but nothing.

On that evening you desire to declare, in the very act of baptism, that he has answered your cry, the one that book calls *He*.

Come to think of it, you, too, needed many years to find words ample and clear enough to express what you had already lived but could not say. As though anybody can say it.

Unless maybe in the words of that ancient, untenable prayer directed, no less, to someone who has "fathomed my heart and knows me."

It was my good fortune, these past months, to hand these words on to you. Just as I, too, received them from others, the words of psalm 139:

"You have fathomed my heart, O God, and you know me,
    my God, you know when I come and go;
  you see through my thoughts from afar,
    all that I do is familiar to you,
  yes, and there comes not a word to my lips,
    my God, before it has reached your ear." *

So intense and joyful was your recognition, in those words, of the voice of your voice, that they took on a new splendor and meaning for me. Maybe you are hoping they will take on new splendor and meaning for all of us that evening, as the words of that song are said and sung:

"I am your doing in heart and loins,
    you wove me in my mother's womb,
  I thank you for your wondrous work—
    in me there was nothing hid from your eyes." **

And some phrases from the second song you chose for your baptism:
    "In the beginning
    was the word
    and the word was
    in the presence
    of our God. . . .
    "The word
    has become flesh. . . .

> he alone
> is
> our guide." *

Handed down, these words, by people who recognized in Jesus of Nazareth who *they themselves* are and are not, and what they must do, and what lies ahead for them; and how deeply they are known, and by whom. Jesus is the word casting light along the way of their lives.

To be baptized in his name, to entrust yourself to his name, means to want to guarantee others that his way can be trusted; that "an eye for an eye and a tooth for a tooth" is not the ultimate truth in this universe, but that friendship and forgiveness, gentleness and thirsting-after-justice is the only way to live.

Those who do entrust themselves to his name, who believe in the one in whom he believed, those who do—who dare *do God*—as Jesus did, they shall live anew for others, for and with the nearest neighbors given them, with a predilection for all that is vulnerable, orphaned, poor, and deprived in this world.

"In the Beginning": a song which only succeeds in stirring up, once more, all the questions in the world, and naturally provides no kind of sure answer, easily available once you are baptized. I'll ask you, that evening, whether you want to try to keep that song alive within yourself, in company with us; and you, in turn, must ask us whether we want to try the same with you. I know both you and we will answer "yes," not triumphantly, yet surely full of hope.

Then you will stand up, in the midst of our circle, and you will lower your head, and I shall pour water over you, say-

ing: We baptize you in the name of Jesus, since you wish
to live in his spirit, that you might continue along his way:
in the Name of the Father, and of the Son, and of the Holy
Spirit.

Then I shall make the sign of the cross upon your fore-
head, saying: I sign you with his cross, the sign of the life
he chose; live following after him, to meet his God and
father, and be at peace.

❧ NOW WITH WORDS

Now with words half blurring
far and near
as in a mirror, darkly
not quite clear
we remain strangers who see
and soon forget,
blindly we do what we must
unknowing yet.
Then shall appear
what cannot be:
we shall go open wide
and see and hear, be face to face
and know who was inside.

Knowledge beyond whatever
fear and mask,
and love no meaningless word
but love at last;
body and silence suffice
and just our names
resting in light—the lamb

on the lion's mane.
Love's word is hard
and comes and goes
and comes like death in you.
Who dreams such song until the end?
A man and woman do.

> sung to a melody from the
> *Gedenck-clanck* of Valerius (17th century)

❧ THE STONE AND THE FISH

Once upon a time there was a stone. And once upon a time there was a fish.

"I'm made of flesh," said the fish.

"I'm made of stone," said the stone.

"You should put on a pair of trousers," said the fish, "life is short, and you'll catch cold with no clothes on."

The stone set out on a journey, and bought a pair of trousers made of moss.

The fish wanted to go to school. Now that the stone was still on a journey, and the moss with him, and the woods in his bag, and the beach rolled up on his back, and everything was suddenly so completely different, now the fish wanted to go to school.

"Hello, fish," said the principal, "second row, third bench."

Reading lesson: rose, jewel, banquet, mercedes benz. The fish learned a lot.

Things grew too hard for the stone. Just being rolled around, or thrown, or casually kicked, or called "sissy," or being taken for a tortoise. "What's the use?" he sometimes said to himself.

Once, in the middle of a wheat field, when summer scorched and no wind blew, he decided he had had it. And he came up with the bright idea that he wanted to fly. But he was lonely for the fish. And he knew nothing about the school, the second row, bench, or banquet. What should he do?

The fish received a diploma, after thirteen years, and a pectoral chain, and a marvelous house, and had already been long since married. You could hardly call her a fish now, she had become a star and had forgotten all about the old days.

One time, at the club, the star heard that somewhere in a little backwoods village, there dwelt a stone who could fly. The star set out on a journey.

The stone was lying under a tree, furrowed and ashen, a leaf over him, or at evening the slow gliding light across him. He was poor. He just lay there, thinking a bit, his thoughts short like sighs. But flying? No.

The star saw the stone. The stone saw the star. Then the stone wept, thinking, "All this time I've been waiting, that's what I've been doing. O, whatever made me think I was thinking?"

"You're still a stone," said the star.

"I'll strip off your glassy clothes," said the stone, "or wouldn't you be glad to be a fish again?"

"Yes," said the star.

"Shall we get out," asked the stone, "head over heels, through the dark void? Shall we beat it, out of this cave?"

"Yes," said the star, who had already taken off her hat.

Off they went, she first. Against the rising wind. And so it came to pass that hands slowly began to grow where once there had been only diamond fins.

SONG TO THE HOLY SPIRIT
("Veni Sancte Spiritus,"
9th century, freely translated)

Breathe here, now, and kindle me,
send me from your farthest distance
surging light.

Welcome, poor folk's father
welcome, chief cupbearer
welcome, hunter of hearts.

Gentlest dryer of tears
loving soul-indweller
my friend, my shadow.

Restful moment
for drudgers and toilers
and breathing-spell for spastic kids, are you.

Impossibly lovely light,
overflow the abyss
which you know so well—my heart.

You are God, without you
only night, untimely time,
violence and guilt.

You make me clean,
you soothe my wounds,
give water to my withered flower.

I stand stiff, read NO ADMITTANCE,
am icebound—melt, embrace me;
I go astray, come seek me.

I tell you Yes, do No—
repay my doubt with friendship
seven times a thousand times.

Without you I am nothing.
Dead, I would go to you.
Then, I'll be laughing!

❧ WHO THE SINGERS ARE

I saw a mighty gathering
whose total none can tell
all called together
from every continent and language.
They stood before the throne
of him who lives,
encircling the lamb.
They all were arrayed
in streaming white.
They were singing, with towering voices,
exulting:
"Blessed be our God, the living one
and blessed be the lamb!"
I asked:

"Those there, the singers,
all dressed in streaming white,
who are they?"
Someone said to me:
"There you see
all those who've gone through hell."

Then I saw the dead
standing round the throne,
the great and the small.
The sea yielded up all her dead.
And death and the chasm
gave up their dead, gave them back.

a vision of John,
Revelations 7:9–17
freely rendered

TO BELIEVE IN SOMETHING SO SMALL and irreplaceable as a song. I'm all for what the old ads say: "A Wide Variety of Favourite Songs, Olde and New—Whereby You May Dispel Melancholie and Sadness!" I would want songs more artless, sweet, wistful and wise than most people are.

To sing as a way of communicating; to treat people in such a way that you lead them back to what is simple and fundamental in themselves.

To sing with others; to cast off your embarrassment and cynicism, to become a little exposed and unashamed, one with another; every voice good enough, no human being too small to join in.

Could I hope to win you with a song
    I'd be content I'm born;
I would think and work and write it
    late at night and early morn.*

To win people to each other, with songs.

ONCE THERE WERE TWO PEOPLE. One could sing, the other could listen. When the one sang about a tree, the other said: I see a tree . . . blooming in the desert . . . we are resting in the shadow of its branches. When the one sang about the other, the other said: I am you.

❧ OF THE ONE AND THE OTHER

Before I saw trees
the hazel in bloom or in winter
the holm oak or chestnut
I saw you.

Little sister, my love
my distant friend,
my heart is yours,
little neighbor, what have I done
to you, and you to me?

Before the sea called me,
as smooth as glass, then churning back,
before the polestar or the calm,
you called me.

I bought a flute and fluted
a veil of fire all round you,
one body more, facing
the long portage.

If I should ever come upon
some wells or mines or words
more deep than these,
I want you there.

Little sister, my love
my distant friend,
my heart is yours,
little neighbor, what have I done
to you, and you to me?

TO SING CONTAGIOUSLY: catching fire from each
other. That is what I want to see, and to experience.

"And they sang, in panic and pain. Everything drifted
back. And everything seemed so long ago, and you longed
for something, once again, but what was it? And you
longed for somewhere, anywhere."
        —lines from *Heimwee* (Homesickness), by Nescio*

To sing what you are; what you live, and have lived so
long, laboring, taciturn, dazed, lonely, not knowing, jab-
bering, stammering; your town, your hands, your questions, your wife, your friend, your voice, your past, your
paltry future-here-and-now.
    To make yourself (or another) the least bit more ac-

quainted with another (or yourself). To recapture pure
words, purifying the air.

Training in waiting, humming, listening, being silent.
Training in imagination, feeling, ecstasy.

By doing, to become greater than you are.

ᵛᵉ OF FIRE AND IRON
(*melody: a Polish folkdance*)

Of fire and iron, of biting brine
as wide as light, as old as time
mankind is everything combined
   and born anew each morning.
To be that iron in fire,
to be both salt and sweet and sour,
share people's tears and their desires—
   for this are people born.

To be the water for the sea,
to be the word that makes man free,
become what no one can foresee—
   sought out, esteemed, forgotten;
be evening-and-morning land,
be here—yet in the great beyond,
to dare take hold of someone's hand
   and never be abandoned.

To be as old and wide as light,
be mouth, be food, be appetite,
be everything, yet be a mite—
   for this, one seeks the other.
Toward outlands no one can discern

through fire that forges people firm—
to live the bitter and the sweet
   we go to one another.

A SHORT SONG (a motto, watchword, theme song) heard rising from the circle of the first followers of Jesus of Nazareth. Distilled faith. A clarion call, and a promise:

Wake up now, sleepy head,
rise-from-death rise-from-death
a brand new man, like light
must rise in you.

Words to savor, a dream to sing inside you. As long as we sing, we know.

I believe in believing songs, which contain words that can only be sung, which know what cannot be known, are defenseless as only songs can be.

To sing: a delicate balance of words and wordlessness, of speaking and silence.
   To establish centers of freedom where that art can be acquired, transmitted, preserved. Schools for freely expressed interiority.

❧ YOU ARE

You are the God
who has been given me,
the cup

which stands brimful for me;
my lot in life
rests in your hand, good land
is my
appointed portion.

You are the lot
which has befallen me,
my shadow,
the angel who consoles and racks—
then let this chalice
be quick to pass me by,
I blanch
at drinking people.

Who are you,
you that bid me come and drink?
You waver
still at my door, you knock and wait;
or like the thirsting stag
and I the stream run dry
thirsting
for teeming rainfall.

SINGING: because you are talked out, knocked out. Because you are sad, and want to be cheered up. Huddled together at the wailing wall, crying *help, help,* are all those who cannot save themselves. Singing songs of guilt and fear, frustration and longing. Psalms out of the depths; inside the belly of the monster; in ghettos and gas chambers. Or fixed to a stake: Why have you forsaken me? That's real singing. To sing against overwhelming odds. Against invisible foes. Against the deadly fire of plain facts. Against the flames, and up out of the flames: a song in the fiery furnace.

In the bible we are told how three mere men endured the furnace, stood up in the white-hot core of the fever we call life; and how they were reduced to a song, and to the vision of a new creation, a new man, a living God. That trio is every man who has remained upright and has not resigned himself to his slavery. All who have dreamed and envisioned a life which endures and has a future.

❧ FOUR WALLS *

Four walls and a roof of reed
not a bit more not a bit more.

A robin hiding in the reed
I am no more I am no more

and he who hunts me finds me not
and he who shoots me wings me not.

Three walls around a stalk of reed
not a bit more not a bit more.

The eastern wind, it breaks me not
the western wind uproots me not

the winds may rise the winds may fall
firm stands my stalk against them all

of scent and color I have none
I bend but break I have not done.

Two walls of intertwining reed
not a bit more not a bit more.

Through my thin rushes wind has blown,
cried through the marrow of my bones

who weeps for me has failed to grasp
who seeks my shelter shall not last

for scent and color I have none
I almost break, and yet I don't

I have a crest that sways and stirs
above the strangest flock of birds.

The flames engulf the roof of reed
one wall remains, not a bit more.

A heap of stones and blackened grass
a bird who smoulders in the trash

the winds from east and west and south
fan every spark and blow them out

four three two walls, and then but one
only the wind around me now

but he who hates me knows me not
and he who hits me hurts me not

a swaying crest a spark a song
not a bit more not a bit more.

SINGING PASSES DOWN THE DREAM of man as he was meant to be. Passes down the lament: Man, now where are you, when will you be man at last? Passes down the hope: There is a door standing open which no one can close; someone has said, "I am the door." (It is a stage door painted on a blind wall, you think, at least once in every song.)

A song is, itself, a door standing open; usually just ajar, sometimes open wide. In the midst of quiet drudgery and despairing protest, I try singing to keep my conscience open to the vision of a different order: weapons melted down, people who no longer train for battle.

Slaves shall dream dreams; prisoners shall have visions.

❧ TREES DON'T SCREAM OUT

Trees don't scream out, nor earth nor branches,
the sea does not weep, nor the birds nor the town.
No cry from the mouths of the city walls,
only the laughing star's alarm.

Only in man has a mouth been cut,
heart plunked in so he might weep,
lips contorted, dark and aghast.
Man and woman: hit your heads against the wall

against murder and night and the chrome-plated
engines of the holy war,
against the law of terror
wasting whatever is small.

Now there, now elsewhere, but always here
the mother weeps for her sons
the just man mourns his brothers
because they are no more.

In people a spring, a volcano is crying,
man for his kind, a quaking with shame
that dead or alive we do not
turn in this hour into peace.

FROM LONG AND APPALLING EXPERIENCE the bible knows how people act toward each other in real life: the blind who lead the blind, and those who teach each other warfare. But hoping against hope, there are always those people, the castaways, the missing, the hounded, who go on dreaming the impossible dream, singing it till today: *You have a future.* Who, I? Yes, you. Squarely at me, the songs of the bible sing: *You are that man.*

If one blind man leads another, both will end in a pit.
—Mt. 15:14

❧ OF TODAY AND TOMORROW

No language renders him
no song comes close to him
no god can equal him.
His hands play into
every new beginning,
no other bears us up.
He who spoke in silences,
breaking the bonds of fate
and opening up new ways
is not dumbfounded yet;
he seeks and comes to meet us
in people, one by one.

Most things pass away
but he is more and more
the future that awaits us,
he plumbs and tries out hearts.
We do not really live,
we view his land of rest
and justice from a distance.
A desert rings us round
and one by one we all
estrange, fall down, and die.

When all things are fulfilled
then he shall be our city,
a city of bread and games.
The rod that rules us now
and tongue that cuts us down
and death shall be no more.
His light along our veins

will shine forth from our eyes,
our past will be complete.
Our daydreams will come true:
we'll speak to one another
the language of hope and peace.

TO SING TO EACH OTHER, to sing each other to account, to enlarge someone with a birthday song: "l-o-n-g
may you live, l-o-n-g may you live"—and you grow confused, being celebrated like that, openly. To sing color
into each other, to make someone shine, and glow, and
beam; to sing someone open. To sing God open, toward
you, overflowing his banks. Sing, then, like rivers joined in
song for God: long may he live.

One time someone dreamt that there were places where he
was welcome. But they were widely separated. Like hot and
cold. In a glass helicopter, he journeyed from one to the
other, and always, upon landing, he heard singing. But he
couldn't catch the words, so beside himself was he with
pride and joy. Because he thought: they are singing for me.
    Awake again, half out of bed, running his fingers
through his hair, he imagined that he remembered the
words, after all. He dressed, ate his breakfast, and began
to write.

❧ SONG OF THE JOURNEY

Here it comes, a nameless child
from somewhere far away and wild;
it's no one yet, it speaks no word,

of death it hasn't even heard,
still crying from the pain of birth,
who knows who it may be on earth?

Then people cry out, "Hi, there, hi
live here with us, be at my side,
the world shall be a home for you
and love will make you human, too."

We dub each other with a name:
someone no one
child of Adam
are you proclaimed.

Heading somewhere on his own,
a man must walk his way alone,
must seek in wilderness somewhere
if living water ripples there,
and listen if there is a word
in which his future may be heard.

Then people cry out, "Hi, there, hi
live here with us, be at my side,
the water leaps up high for you,
the future has a word for you."

And then a man finds out his name:
someone no one
thirst and water
child of Adam
are you proclaimed.

His "wherefore" no one understands—
just why he has a heart and hands;

the why's and wherefore's are unknown,
we're so much breath and blood and bone.
A man lives on, and waits his fate,
outside so small, inside so great.

Then people cry out, "Hi, there, hi
be heart and hand and man for me,
be why-and-wherefore, great or small,
the man that only you can be."

A man lives on from name to name:
someone no one
thirst and water
friend and stranger
child of Adam
are you proclaimed.

No one knows what life may be
but only that it's given free
from city-dump to golden throne
alike to prince and those unknown.
Whoever lives creates his song,
the others never do catch on.

Let people cry, "Live here with me"
to live, sing out until you're free.
Whoever lives creates his song,
the others never do catch on.

So let us sing each other's name:
someone no one
thirst and water
friend and stranger

dead and living
humankind
are we proclaimed.

TO WANT TO SPEAK as "in the beginning": as a man speaks with his friend, face to face. To want to be a word "in the presence of God," unashamed and patiently turned toward him, unprotected and unthreatened. To cherish and hold on to that passion for a hearing and for silence which is called "praying."

To believe, against all the scoffers, all the ears that hear not, that it is, in fact, possible both to speak and to be like this; that it is an art; that more than an abstract idea worth dying for, it is a genuine human prospect, worth living for. Because one time, someone did live like this, in the midst of people: "the word in the presence of God" became flesh. It has already happened, right here in this kingdom of earth. He was seen, heard, touched, one time.

Songs are written to come to fruition: a gravestone rolled away from my mouth; an icecap melted off us.

❧ AND THEN *

From status, standing, wisdom battered loose.
overturned. uprooted sycamore.
it felt light spreading then beneath its bark.
a spray of buds about to blossom forth.

Fled now from friends and from my waning words.
hunted somewhere past the timber line,
I catch my breath in thinning air, I hear
my own heart beating: outlaw, bird set free.

From my own self at last toward someone else,
bound to seek each other evermore,
till I find Him and He finds me. And then!
a sea of dreams is raging in my heart.

for Piet Ahsmann

✌ TOO FEW ARE THE PLACES

To be unable to get a word in. Or to come to light. To be possessed by the demon muteness. To be snuffed out. Or never to have a good word to say.

Synonyms for one and the same experience, the lot of almost everyone.

A world full of TV antennas, broadcasting towers, communiques, and live audiences; yet a wordless world: of pent-up rage, blind fear, smooth-talking, and oblivion.

Words keep us alive. I would be lost; I would wither away or dissolve in my own chaos, crushed beneath the silent majority and wordless violence, were I no longer to express who I am. Whoever gives up expressing himself and others, will never get a word in any more, will get lost, will become nameless. He will go silent majority himself.

Words—from yes to no, from cry-of-fear to word-of-honor and one's own name, from cursing to conversation—words are the very light of life for human beings. To be able to speak is to have a chance for the future and for mutual recognition.

But the juridical world-order we worship gags and censors that chance for life, eclipses the real word. People who speak true words are sure, at the very least, to be frozen out, laughed off, ostracized, rendered suspect, or just ignored to death. To this day, the darkness has never been able to stand the light.

In exposed and perilous places, so easy to drown out, there are people still trying to speak, to hear, and to be heard. There are some people trying, as of old, to restore that very first requirement of living humanly together.

In the face of a wordless babbling world, to try to create a place where people can, perhaps, gain a hearing from each other. To show that it is possible for people to understand each other, that they are not doomed to compounded misjudgments. A vocation. An art.

To transmit *people* to people. People of old to people of now. In the hope that this will see something new happen: the shock, the joy, of recognition. One's own questions, intimations, feelings recognized in this person or that. Thrilling to another. A meshing recognized. Behold, the man, you are that man: he is like me, it is up to me, and always, us.

Too few are the places where people, generally mere shadows of themselves, grow into living images, recognizable to each other; where the art (and strategy) of mutual enlightenment is practiced, and the effort is to come clear; where people truly look into and interpret each other, help each other to get their bearings. So that people can see themselves, as it were, pass in review, and heartened by this new insight, can set out upon their way once more.

Places are needed where people are wholeheartedly dedicated to the proposition that *something* remains to be seen. That at times, and ever again, something can come to the light of day which makes all the bother of looking, straining, deciphering, unraveling signs, the tears, the doubting and waiting—worthwhile.

In the midst of piles of printed words I sit, I think. At the window of my TV I sit, I look at people who nearly touch me, so alarmingly close yet impossibly far away. Do they really exist?

Horrors, large and small, pepper my eyes. But it hurts less each time. First dumbfounded, then somewhat dulled, and from now on more merciless each time, I go on looking. Until I don't even see it any more. As was foretold by the prophet, "though ten thousand fall down before your eyes, it will not touch you." People are falling, more and more, outside the reach of my heart. Neither their joy nor their misery can find me any more. Nor mine them. Everybody knows everybody else's misery, already. In advance. To gain the whole world, but to lose your own soul. That's what it's called.

I'm looking for a place where I might get a little closer to what happens next to me, far away, in myself. Where, together with others perhaps, I might be able to feel again, find the time, grieve, console and be consoled, see and be seen. Where I can stand existing.

I am looking in the heart of the city where I live (don't live, go astray, flee, get lost) for one or another house. With some small and some large rooms, cozy nooks, open fireplaces, large closets, windows which look out upon trees, balconies, a garden with a small pavilion. Where, as at a center of communications, all kinds of questions and experiments (mystical, political, whatever) could connect, and reinforce each other.

A place for varied forms of expression, strange and familiar. For people of every stripe and time of life: for the very old, for Portuguese and Russian refugees, readers of poems, musicians out of a job. A house like a living body, a matrix of functions. Symbol and promise and (again, but no accident) a small beginning of that life-style, way of speaking and feeling and getting on with yourself and others which is called friendship. A place where patient effort is made to break through the isolation in which everyone, churched or unchurched, believer or not, run-of-mill or genius, crone or crown princess is imprisoned.

A house where someone is welcome when he is welcome nowhere else. Where, wandering by, he may perchance read above the entrance—

Hello, it's mighty good to see you here
welcome voices, new and old, the pure, the high, the low
welcome strangers, every blesséd soul
here you are, your teeth sunk into "now"
welcome, dreams about tonight, you dusky mirrors
unreadable omens
those scrawny cows who ate the fat ones up
the withered grain that gobbled down the full
whatever you may mean, warm welcome, visions
welcome twanging strings and bows and bongos
flutes and eardrums, beating pulses
ivories black and white, pedals soft and loud
welcome, creaking wood and crinkling clothing
all that makes a noise because it lives
stray swallow, welcome, and last blue crane
dying sea gull
welcome, friendship, twine like a streamer

of eyes and hands around us
a garland of roses and thorns
welcome, love, godsend from heaven
welcome, everyone, and listen now
come be my bread and I'll be your wine
hello, it's really good to see you here

Are there hidden places, inner chambers, left hands which don't know what the right is doing? Are there really people who withdraw from publicity, what others think, a show of strength, and gaze honestly into themselves? To become like a child, to be born again, to lose your life—that's what the gospel calls it. Praying. The foolishness and frailty of God. Not a paying proposition, no market for it. To do what cannot be done: remembering the dead, cherishing hunger and homesickness, fasting.

Hidden places, where a sad man is safe. Show yourself to the world—leap down from the roof of the temple—come down from your cross: thus they cried to him. Those who believe (go on being trustworthy) are hidden with him in God. Is there a God, a Father who sees in secret? Is there anything beyond what can be seen, heard, measured? Would just one word, spoken, written, lived in truth, however hidden it might be, accomplish something, work contagiously, set someone glowing? I once read, only hidden things give support.

Hidden places, just large enough for two or three together. The gates of hell, the powers of the Kingdom of Death, all those gods-of-people who stand entrenched, the law and the money and no-shadow-of-a-doubt on their side—none of them can cope with what is hidden, much less prevail against it.

Churches which bless the measurable, prevailing order, defend compulsory military training, own shares in war industries, support colonial powers, and whose leaders dwell in palaces, dispatching emissaries—they have long since been prevailed against by the gates of hell. But they do not know it. They know not what they do.

❧ A HUNDRED FLOWERS

Let a hundred flowers blossom,
earth and air enough for endless
tubers, seeds, and pink carnations;
stones are stones and must remain so,
people soar aloft like godlings,
but let shamrocks and the clover
blossom forth a hundredfold!

Cornflowers blue as bits of
heaven, poppies glow like gashes,
morning stars along the sluiceways
coaxing to be seen by someone;
growing rampant in the poplars
mistletoe entwines and nestles,
spray of kisses bittersweet.

On his thorny stalk the balding
squire is blooming and is grieving
and no butterfly will find him;
trunks of trees shall bring forth branches,
ferns engraved on frozen panes shall
flutter, and a hundred paper
roses yet shall come to bloom.

Fragile, still with stems unbroken,
these entangled wild and blindly,

those in caverns or on dung-heaps,
others pressed by ice or pages,
or on tombstones—let a hundred
very different independent
nameless flowers come to bloom!

In a woods of dreamy jungle,
stony roots and wiredrawn cobwebs,
labyrinth of words all whirling
dwells a man, a spindly bungler,
lily of the field, his eyes grown
misty, nearly blind with looking
for a spot beside a spring.

❧ UNLESS A MIRACLE HAPPENS

about
  — *the incurable nostalgia for leaders and strong men*
  — *the vision of a different world-order: "everybody or
    nobody"*
  — *believing; the discernment of spirits; choosing life;
    being restless*

Would we not, in fact (who is *we?* how many?), would we
not be very happy to have:
  a modern saint, a great (preferably invisible) ensouler,
our own Marx, a pluri-dimensional Marcuse?
  an international prize-beast, a man from Mars, yet still
a man of flesh and blood, with a beautiful woman up his
sleeve?
  or preferably, safer: a team of new Marx's and Marcuse's, popes, men from Mars, saints, thinkers, inventors,
wise men from the East and managers from the West?

Yes, exactly. Because things are going badly with our world. We have only about thirty years left on our planet. Unless a miracle happens.

> "And filled with an incurable nostalgia
>   to see the King for whom I longed to fight,
>   I strode toward Death." *

Lines from a famous poem of Hendrik Marsman, early in this century. From the time between the two world wars, when democracy was everywhere grown sick, and the cry went up for strong men.

Hendrik Marsman was very popular in that period. His first volume, in its red cover, was known among the litterati of the day as "the red book."

He never did see his "King," and that is to his credit. Because, since the time he wrote those lines, there have been plenty of kings-führers-duces-strongmen, and millions have strode in their name toward Death. And yet, that incurable nostalgia for a king, a strong man, has persisted.

In that generally invisible, silent, oppressed, and confused majority, everywhere and nowhere, it keeps turning up, like a ghost, that dream of a saviour.

Deep in his soul, every man dreams that dream a little. And in the most varied relations between people—friends, lovers, father and son, teacher and pupil, doctor and patient—that incurable nostalgia keeps working. That nostalgia for someone with a golden key in one hand and the philosopher's stone in the other, someone unique, who pulls the chestnuts out of the fire for you; or who tells you, gently, "Now you just go off to sleep."

Every religion of the world testifies to it, that people

want supermen: wonder-workers; a great guru: a universal teacher; our much-esteemed Chairman Mao, the Shining Sun; Jesus Christ Superstar; a Hail Miss Universe. We want to venerate, exalt, rave about, worship—we people do. We erect statues for generals and admirals, and pay the annual TV tax to look at heart-transplanters and other slick artists and stars who have made it (and who, with their aura of importance and success, put you in the shade; you sit and wish you were like them, knowing you are not, knowing you are, perhaps, even nothing).

We cry out for spiritual leaders, gods and heroes: Give us a king! Why?

Because we are so small? Because every man is, after all, a bungler, and no one can save himself? Because this world is a chaos of seething people; a jungle of carniverous plants and dead-end roads; a labyrinth of low blows, slogans, ambivalent feelings, intrigues, and brilliant ideas? So many things exist, so much happens, and surely everything must have something to do with everything else; but one senses no pattern, only rampant growth and loneliness.

I'll never find my way in such an unlivable world, you think then. And naturally, you become dejected and just put in time, listlessly. Thousands and thousands around you are doing the same; what else can we do?

And then, by a lucky stroke of fate, a chance in a lifetime, a godsend (some say), you run into someone who sees something more in the whole business; who has a plan, a direction; who gives calm counsel amid the chaotic mass of meaningless events. Someone who knows the way a little in this jungle, and says, "Look out, that's a swamp; but over here, where I walk, the way is firm." Someone who knows: this is edible, that is poison.

When you meet such a person, you dash off and call

some other bunglers, of course, and you say: "I have found the saviour." And all of you (12? 72? 3000?) gather round him, and he tells you what has to be done. He assigns you a task, motivates you; he makes decisions, takes responsibility; he sets things in order, and when necessary, sets all of you in order of battle, so you can slash through the lines.

He becomes your point of reference. You look up to him. You invest all your capital of talents and hope in him. You develop an iron-clad attachment to him, and not only you, but so do the others.

All around him the jungle turns into a livable world; a meaningful pattern begins to emerge. And he himself, the leader, the king, the high-priest (or whatever title you choose to confer upon him), he embodies that pattern in himself. He is the pattern, in his very own person, the guarantee of the new livability. As long as you cling closely to him, you are part of the pattern, you belong, you are part of the whole. And what more could you want, as a human being?

And his sayings, the wise laws he has given, the experience of life which he has recounted—you must drink deeply of all that. It must pound and sing in your head and in your hands. Consequently, you all begin to recite his words, out loud. It becomes a powerful ritual: an untold mass of Chinese, all waving Mao's little red book in their hands (or, in ten years, some other little book). Or St. Peter's square, jammed with pilgrims, all loudly acclaiming the pope.

Dear pope, poor brother Montini, poor Mao, poor anybody who is so saddled with power and responsibility for the whole universe, for everything and everybody in it—

high up there on your horses. Poor kings, leaders, high-priests, or whatever you're called. Poor anyone who is idolized by people and weighed down beneath the long-ings and illusions of others. Poor strong man. You will give way under the weight which everybody pushes off on you. All blind hostilities, every disappointment will make you their target. You will be blamed for the bondage, im-potence, and failure of others; and naturally, you will have only yourself to blame.

Because people have expected everything of you, they will reproach you with everything. Any psychiatrist can explain that to you, from his own experience.

Or you'll become corrupt, the way every king always be-comes corrupt. The way no less than David of Israel proved untrustworthy, when the chips were down: a hireling who takes the ewe lamb from the poor man, for himself.

Poor mighty-of-the-earth, choking on your own power. "Each other's underlings, imprisoned in our dreaming, that's us . . . such are we." And what seemed a pattern shall prove but chaos, after all, a jungle; even as our era's millenium, the Third Reich, lay in ruins just twelve years after it was ushered in—and beneath it, millions of little people. Yet the nostalgia for a king, a strong man, remains incurable. It is evident, everywhere, and always again, and very likely in us, too.

"In those days," in the declining years of Samuel, the last of the Judges, Israel was in chaos. In fact, there was no "Israel" at all, no unified people. Scattered here and there in that long-awaited, finally-gained, so-called Promised Land, there was a rash of small tribes, clans, villages, and mini-towns, but not a people, no unity; and certainly no justice—everyone did whatever he pleased. Once there were Judges among them, among those children of Israel and descendants of that exodus-people. But in their extreme need, when they could expect nothing any more from each other, God "raised up" a charismatic leader: Deborah, Gideon, Jephthah, Samson. People who did not arrogate leadership to themselves through man-made intrigues, or by succession, but who, in spite of themselves, are burdened with the impossible task: to keep alive the vision of the God of the dispossessed, to establish justice, to preach disbelief in the iron laws of nature and of fate, and to personally embody that disbelief.

They answer the call which is theirs, then quietly leave the scene. The people beg Gideon: "Rule over us, your son and your grandson." Gideon replies, "Neither I nor my son shall rule over you, but He shall rule over you."

In the prophetic Book of Judges, these proto-heroes and bruisers, these strong men, are sketched with telling, almost malicious, pleasure, unmasked as wavering, ambivalent people who have good reason to depend entirely upon "the spirit of God," and who are, in their own right, just as much duds as the powers against whom they are ranged. One after the other gets entangled in his own stupidities: Samson, the strongest of all, falls prey to his erotic escapades.

"Give us a king!" they cried in Israel "in those days," when justice was no more and worship declined and enemies invaded at will. Give us a king who will win our wars and guarantee our status as a nation.

Something like saying: give us a god like a bull, a potent god with genitals of gold, who gets something done, who guarantees fertility, assures profits and prosperity—is there anything wrong with wanting that?

"Give us a king." You shall be slaves, Samuel replies. Your king shall harness your strong and handsome sons to his chariots, and close up your daughters in his harem. He shall require a court, done up with visors and epaulets—not to mention ladies-in-waiting, a crown, a flag, assorted favorites, classes and ranks, a dynasty. And he will pour money into it—whose money? "The warm were warmed/ the poor made poorer." *

The non-entities will be kicked upstairs. The olive tree, the fig tree, the vine will not be available to become King of the Trees, a famous parable says, but rather the bramble, that idler, who bears no fruit and casts no shadow, offers no shelter and bursts in a flash into flame, destroying the cedars of Lebanon.

You shall be prey to a highly flammable regime: the fire of rebellion and anarchy can destroy such leadership at any moment.

"Give us a king." And they got their king, one after the other.

And after Samuel, all the prophets, those bearers of the voice, will say it again: It was not that you might be as other peoples or each other's underlings that He has brought you out of Egypt, but that you might stick together, like fellow-travelers; a body with hands and feet and a head—

> now the hand
> now the foot
> does what is good and must be,
> for none in this land
> is king for good
> no one is god
> not one.

There it stands, apodictic, tendentious, if you will: no one. When someone tells you: Here he is, or there—do not believe him. All of them are hirelings, shepherds who tend themselves.

For the sake of all, says the Voice, for the sake of widows and orphans, for the sake of the strangers in your midst, for the sake of all that is defenseless and can be demolished with one blow, for the sake of the human community itself —do not make gods of each other.

It is not the man in power who is the focus, beginning, and end: Do not serve him "as to the eye," says the prophet, the Voice, but dare to look into the eyes of the poor.

The psalms describe an alternative strong man, a king who stands up for the dispossessed. In those same psalms, the voice of Israel's conscience echoes. And that conscience is so irreducible to whatever philosophical intuition that, in the language of prophecy, God himself has planted it, like a new heart in his people.

In that conscience is rooted the vision of a different world-order, which takes shape and draws near in-the-flesh and becomes credible in the "prince of peace," who is the very opposite of a strong man.

He is a child—what could be more defenseless? He is clothed with the spirit of insight, faithfulness, and patience. He is the one who is prepared to post bond for others. He serves to bring all together. He bears our burdens, the prophet Isaiah says.

He is without figure or splendor, like a twig on an uprooted trunk. Scorched and withered waste land, ruined, thirsty, from which a small shoot comes forth, a green bit of nothing, formless, no beauty in him. But upon him rests, in the vision of the prophet, the power of the spirit of God. In him dwells the fullness, all-of-God, he *is* God-of-the-poor.

He *is* the deprived for whom he stands up. He shall bring it to completion. Bring what? The world that is upside down. "O high and mighty, you shall stand dumbfounded, wide-eyed and open-mouthed, as if you beheld water burning," the prophet Isaiah says in the Song of the Servant.*

Jesus of Nazareth. His followers have recognized in him the prince of peace, the child, the servant. The alternate strong man. The Messiah. In whom the God of the poor permits himself to be known: God. Those who called him thus knew, more fiercely than I can imagine, that he died the death of a slave.

The Servant, the prince of peace, will have insight, the prophet Isaiah foretells, will know what it means to be not a "god," not nothing, but a man. He will learn it in his flesh. At the hands of people. Immersed, baptized (nearly drowned) in that sea of people. He will be called to account, sentenced, expelled, slandered, ignored to death: a man of afflictions, a lamb led to the slaughter; and he will take it, see it through, because he knows.

Knows what? His destiny, his "name." Who he is, and where he is going. No demigod, with wings on his heels. No goddess with snakes in her hair. No miraculous bird, who on wings of dreams can escape the hard facts.

But not simply lost in the crowd. Nor powerless-and-sinful-by-nature, born a victim, once and for all the underling of "the course of nature," fate, the blowing of the wind, the rising and the setting of the sun, the status of the stars, the status quo.

A man of flesh, fragile as a flower. But a man among men, and reaching toward someone else. "Woven in the womb of the earth," a psalm says, woven into all that lives. A man with ears. Approachable, responsive. A freedman. Created to grow, across God knows what boundaries, to leap God knows what limits. Called to choose—for life or for death.

> "I call heaven and earth today
>   to witness against you:
>   I have set before you life and death,
>   the blessing and the curse;
>   choose life, then, that you may live,
>   you and your descendants" *
>   —says Moses, the prophet of prophets.

To choose death: "Why should I be responsible? Who am I? I have no name, not me! How could *I* ever hope to break the fatal iron circle of cause-and-effect, impotence, guilt heaped on guilt, everyman's guilt? Anyhow, what have I to do with anyone else? Am I my brother's keeper? And besides, I wouldn't know where to begin."

To choose life. To join the human enterprise known as people. To want to be part of a bond which includes everything conceivable, and inconceivable. To want to belong to this one and that, and God knows to what, to every single one of them. In a bond with no ending. To accept the consequences and entanglements; to bear with those inevitable complications. Without pretensions, with eyes wide open, with a passion.

Is "God" a word for that enterprise? Is it he who founds this bond, creates it, intends and guarantees it, whose hope it is that people may be human toward each other, a human-world-without-end? Is he the voice who leads me to my place and task, in that bond?

In that endless mass of people—I scarcely know where to begin—I find someone next to me, somebody or other, and still others, who call to me, abruptly, who look at me. Do they need me? like me? support me? need my support? Are they, somehow, like me? Not galley slaves condemned by fate, but people. People of God?

The prophet in Israel sees through and unmasks the cry for a strong man as a disastrous dream at the expense of the poor, as an effort to escape that interminable enterprise/bond, and thus, one's own responsibility.

The prophet is also the seer of the incredible. He believes that every human being is unique and indispensible in that immeasurable bond, and equipped to choose what is good. Well made, very well made. That, fragile though he is, the human being has the strength to share what he has with another, to be a focal point of goodness, a beginning of justice and peace.

What wonderful words. The prophet believes that they are more than words.

He believes that people can be purified-to-peace. That they are able to discover, as they get their bearings, whether they are on a journey to life, or headed for a dead end.

He also believes that some few can be called upon to make good for others. To keep bright, with their faith and courage, the outlook which has been dimmed by the discouragement of so many.

People who walk into the fray unarmed, uncrowned, without title or commission or delegation, disowned if need be, and who simply say "I" and "you," and try to be a reliable starting point for others, so that they can believe their own eyes; in spite of everything, it is possible to choose for life.

The bible is the story of people who have made that choice. The prophet is the seer of those untold "hidden ones": the humble who are willing to suffer for their choice; who "take up their cross" and walk the way of sacrifice, as it is called in the prophecies and gospels. In the figure of the Servant, all those hidden people are sketched; in him their power and their secret have been magnified and personified. His first followers called Jesus of Nazareth "the servant."

Incurable nostalgia: a few centuries after his death, he has become the Byzantine Christ, impervious and unapproachable, "divine," ruling from his cross; a Judge, a King upon his throne, with the index finger of his right hand pointing significantly toward himself: I am He, to whom all power has been given, and in whom all the Princes of the Church will find their prototype. The Founder of Christianity, and the strong man of the Jesus People. And the answer to every question. Once and for all.

More ancient, and based on a better understanding of the oldest testimonials to him, is a quite different vision, in which, like all prophets, he points, rather, *away* from himself. In this vision, he points people toward each other, and, as though he were God, he is not interested in himself but in that poor person, there, whom even the dogs disdain. Here is a Jesus who has come not to be reverenced but to serve, to efface himself, to be the least, as little seen as God.

The memory of the way in which he regarded himself has come down to us, for example, in his words; "it is good for you that I go away." It is not his visible presence, in-the-flesh, which is the final norm and highest good for every man. It is people who are the highest good for one another.

Those who believe in him, that is, those who choose with him for life, through and with and in people, they shall do even greater miracles than he (he has said). Because two or three, or twelve or three thousand people who choose for life, add up to an even greater miracle than one man who does so.

Those who believe seek for each other. They realize that they must share and transmit the vision together, if it would prove, in the long (and short) run anything more than a kind of mysterious rash affecting this or that fanatic.

They form a bond of fellowship and make agreements which commit them to each other.

They do not believe in wonder-workers and strong men. The miracle is their faith in each other. And that they do not believe that appearances and fate and lies have the last word in this world, nor the last word about anyone whomsoever, no matter how puny, deformed, crippled, blind, leprous, or possessed.

They have agreed not to fight for the liberation of themselves alone. They know, with Brecht, that it is a matter of "everybody or nobody, all or nothing, one alone cannot save himself." *

In their mutual union they seek to survive all things. They accept all the consequences of the insight that no one has the sole voice, the run of things, but that everyone has a voice. They seek to create for each other the condition in which everyone can come to raise his voice; perhaps screaming and howling at first, but then, voicing themselves intelligibly and unambiguously.

They begin at the beginning, by using their brains. Discerning spirits. Analyzing facts. Unraveling arguments. Unmasking the half-truths and sophistries which are lord and master of people and opinions and everyday life, aware that you must spot your own hidden servility, begin to see who is actually running your own life. And then, to unhex reality itself.

They do not shrink from hiddenness and the long process of conversion. They know wherein their choice-for-life differs from cut-rate rebellion against the present order and the past; or from the shortsightedness with which some people try to produce, with a wave of the hand, the absolute antithesis of the established order. And they know, from centuries-old experience, that only the maturing and purifying of individual feelings and insights can support that process of changing society and revolution.

But with the vision of absolute justice ever before their eyes, they work on, from moment to moment, toward some more justice for some more people.

They go and live in those crannies where blows are always falling. Professional infiltrators as they are. Called to be immersed in the fate of the most deprived. There was a time, still is, occasionally, when baptism in the Christian churches was the sign of that irrevocable solidarity.

Those who believe are of no use within the mighty system of our world-order. They feel like exiles, uneasy and awkward, within this whole free-enterprising system, which is not a human way of living for the majority of the peoples of the world.

They are restless. Their fire burns down, fast and furious, and they don't think that's the worst thing that can happen. They always reach beyond their powers, and cannot do otherwise, and don't want it otherwise.

∾ NAMING

Food freely shared by the glutton;
softness from hard-handed men.

Water climbed up the volcano.

Came upon fleet-wingéd feet
over the breakers, the cripple.

On the adamant wall of the subway
someone crayoned a heart
and the name of his child.

∾ SONG OF THE SUN *

Eternal you
invisible and far away
I owe you both my silence and my song

my loneliness and my desires
my hunger, all my longings,
for you are God
it all belongs to you
and whether in distress or peaceful
none can call upon you by your name.

You are the nameless one
and good
good is the hand
that made all things that are;
unspeakably good as well
is brother sun
who daily offers us another day
who bursts with beauty
and with shining power
who blinds and overwhelms us
consoles and makes us glad
and gives us life.

And sister moon is also good
so pretty with her stars
which you have spun of heaven;
and good like you
is brother wind
with all his ranging clouds
and weather good and bad and air
in which we live
lowly yet still happy.

I praise you for your gift—
our sister water,
so helpful and so modest

precious and pure,
for brother fire
who soars against the night
laughing and leaping, subsiding,
and for our sister
mother earth
bearing up our feet,
who guides our path
provides us every fruit
and gives us herbs and flowers
all flashing.

And blessed are you, misunderstood
transcendent
for all who, acting out of love for you
are merciful,
for all the sick and long-enduring thirsty,
and blessed are all the persevering
never crowned
their whole life long—
will you proclaim them?

And cursed, misunderstood
are you
yet still blessed
for her, our sister
the death of the body,
no living soul
can possibly escape her,
and blessed are all
who seek for you;
the second death
shall never overcome them.

Farewell to all, and bless and thank
your Lord and God,
recall him and serve him
in meekness.

> *based on Il Cantico al Sole*
> *of Francis of Assisi*

❧ A STORY

God wanted out of it all, for a week. To see some creatures and how they were doing. He talked it over with
Elijah.

"I'll borrow your long hair and your leather belt and
your name," he cried, "just for a week. Okay?"

"Okay," said Elijah, "but that won't help you; they'll
all recognize you, anyhow."

"Where should I go?" he cried. "Make up a schedule for
me, will you?"

"You might visit the judge, the realtor, the flower-girl,
the ants, the hare, the island. What do you have in mind?"

God gave the matter a lot of thought.

"I can't make up my mind," he finally cried. "You pick
something."

Elijah sent out seven letters, all reading: "Thou shalt
receive a visitor today, someone with long hair and a
leather belt, and his name is Elijah." He scheduled one
visit each day, for seven days.

The judge was not a happy man. He complained about his
back, and he suffered from insomnia. "Small wonder, in
times like these," his wife confided to their friends.

They lived in a house with great high steps, in the
northern part of the country. An old-fashioned bellpull

with a big copper knob stuck out at the entrance. When a visitor pulled it, he heard the echo of the echo.

Deep within sat the judge, brooding over the sentence he had to pronounce on someone who had committed a public something or other.

The mailman rang. It was a sealed letter. The judge read the letter, and thought, "Here comes trouble. He's coming to meddle in this world. That means the end of all jurisprudence and of all morality." He consulted his wife, in a grave voice.

"Well, you could just receive him politely," said his wife, "and no more. . . ."

So they decided not to be at home the following Monday. They did compose a decent, even affectionate greeting, "With sincere regrets." "Heartfelt," suggested his wife. "Sincere," the judge decided.

On Sunday evening, when it was dark, they tied the letter to the bell, like a white flag, and let down the rolling shutters.

Monday morning. "Am I too early, or too late?" thought God. He pulled the bell-knob, carefully, so as not to disturb that little white paper flag. The bell echoed, and the judge and his wife clasped hands (he his own and she likewise), with fingers intertwined, and they both clenched their jaws tightly.

He rang again. And again. "I must not be too forward, at the outset," thought God, as he was tempted to take the letter and read it, out of curiosity. "No," he thought, at the last moment, "whatever has been written for the milkman or the baker, I really should keep my hands off."

"It's a pity," he cried to himself, "I would have liked so much to hear what a judge thinks of this world."

He rang once more, but without hope, and walked at once down the great steps, glanced back, and went his way.

The day wore on. Monday afternoon. God sat at a sidewalk cafe and cried out for a Coke. Just opposite the Cafe Superior stood the offices of the Realtor Bros. of Pennsville. The postman stepped off his bicycle. God saw how the letter of Elijah slipped into the letter-box of the Realtors, and a strong excitement glowed all through him.

Mr. Realtor had enjoyed a beautiful childhood, quite unlike the judge, especially on Sundays, when at High Mass the sun beamed through the stained glass windows and the boys' voices soared from behind his back, rolled over the bowed heads of his father and uncles and great-uncles, singing something so beautiful, something like "Domine, Domine!" No, he was not unaffected by it. However much he doubted later, and gambled and slept around, that memory remained a source of courage in life, of pluck, of much happiness. "Yes, I've always had a soft spot for God," Realtor would say. And his youngest brother backed him up on that, every time. In fact, no spot of land, no little shack was sold, that the two of them did not talk it over thoroughly, in advance.

Together they bent over the letter. "This is a trap," Realtor said, "and I'm not going to get caught in it."

"Elijah?" said the younger brother, "he must be a Protestant from the north, judging by the name."

"I'm flying to Cyprus, tomorrow," said Realtor, "after all, I've been due for a holiday anyhow, for weeks now."

God was consumed by compassion and understanding. He changed a dollar and phoned Elijah, a quarter for three minutes.

"Elijah? Let the sun shine brightly above Cyprus, and if the cabbies are on strike, get a donkey for him, to carry him to his hotel. He really needs a holiday."

When he had hung up, he decided to visit the younger Realtor. "That's something, at least," he thought, "and I'd like to see what a brother is like, whether they resemble each other, and all like that, since I have no brother myself (feeling a twinge of self-pity), unless for Elijah."

Even though the younger Realtor was somewhat different from his brother, he too had taken measures. Near the front door he had posted ENTRANCE IN REAR. God went to the rear.

There stood a storehouse. Not a soul to be seen. But at the doorway of the cinder-block structure stood an antique walnut chest, with seven copper locks. Attached to it was a note: "To God-in-the-form-of-Elijah—from the Realtor Bros., with our apologies—unavoidably absent."

God loved antiques. "Not bad," he thought, "just feel how smooth it is." And while he was lifting up the chest and putting it upon his shoulders, the younger Realtor gave the signal to the eighty-seven photographers, and the hidden cameras clicked away unnoticed. And slowly, with joyful step, God walked on, carefully balancing the great antique upon his back, out of the lenses of the world press, to the left, onto the public road. What a large chest, he himself could fit into it completely, he felt.

Thus he walked, hour after hour. It was a light burden. "But I haven't seen a single creature to talk to, yet," suddenly occurred to him.

"It's because of my long hair," he thought, after walking several more hours, "it scares them off." He took the scissors to his hair, and soon, looking like a freshly plucked chicken, he continued on his way, thinking, "I really love these seven copper locks."

The night wore on, as he walked, and it was Wednesday, his third day on earth.

"Morning, Flower-girl."

"Morning, sir. How dreadful you look!"

"I want to buy flowers, two of each kind."

He bought two roses, two anemones, of every kind of flower, two. And put them in the chest.

"What a lot of buckets you have there," cried God.

"Yes, I do," said the woman. "Are the flowers for a lady?"

"No, they're for heaven," he cried. "Didn't you realize that?"

"No," said the woman.

"I come from heaven," cried God, who had begun to want to make an impression—what a woman!

"From heaven?" she asked.

"Yes," he cried, "through seven spheres of air I have tumbled here. That's why I look so dreadful."

The woman went simply nuts about him.

"If you were God," she said, "you'd get the dearest flower I have. But you're only Elijah."

"Hey," cried God, "I believe my trip is beginning to succeed. Can I take you into my confidence?"

"Anytime," said the flower-girl. She thought of her skirt made all of flowers, at home in the closet: who else had such a skirt? Just her luck, not to have worn it today.

"Now I'll tell you something," cried God. "I know a town that has no offices, no filing cabinets of painted metal, no ringing telephones. You are the first living soul I've ever told about it. We live there on the water, and everything takes place in silence. And babies are not carried about, but flown. And death is not even mentioned."

"Would that mean," asked the flower-girl, who had begun to get cold chills of excitement and to understand more and more, "that the rose there does not prick any more?"

"Yes, exactly," cried God.

A customer came in and bought some roses.

"Do you mean," continued the flower-girl, when she had pocketed the money, "do you mean that it is not dark any more in the hallway, when you come out of the living room in the evening, to go to bed, shuddering and wanting to cry out: 'Is there someone there'?"

"Yes," cried God, "and a lot more, besides."

A couple came along. The judge and his wife. He was leaning on her. They bought irises and narcissi. God's heart was bursting to cry out still more.

"Go on, now, just cry out," said the flower-girl, her arm upon his shoulder, when the couple had walked away, holding the bunches of flowers before them.

"Well," cried God, "you know as much as I do. Who am I, to tell you?"

"Do you mean that, there, you no longer doubt the friendship of your friend?" she asked. "That there, I wouldn't be afraid of you any more, nor you of me? Is that what you mean?"

"Exactly," thought God. But because he suddenly felt the whole thing so impossibly beautiful, he cried instead, "Yes, I mean something like that."

It happened to be World Valentine's Day, and people were crowding around to buy a flower. While wrapping up lilies and chrysanthemums, individually, she told everybody, "Imagine, I had a customer today who said he knows a town where there is no more death."

It was six o'clock in the evening, and everybody was at dinner. In at least a hundred homes, someone was relating how his friend's father had a servant who knew a town where there was no more death.

"No," cried another, "it was my uncle, and it was no more toothache." Everybody thought up and filled in with his own notion of the ideal: no more flat tires, no more strike-outs, every horse in his own stable, the sun and the moon shining forth in the same sky.

It became a great tree of a story. How did you hear it?

From him. And you? From the flower-girl? Flower-girl, how did you come by it? From him. What him? The one with that chest with the seven locks, the one who comes from heaven.

God heard them mumbling, grumbling, quarreling, rejoicing. "I'd better be off," he thought, "before they make me king or lynch me. I've talked too much."

He took up his chest, slunk away, out of the town, into the woods.

"You must not step on us," said the ant, "you'll make one big hospital of it. And you certainly must not step on me, y'see, 'cause I'm the doctor 'round here, and whenever anyone hurts his back on a bit of bark, he comes to me, y'understand?"

"Didn't you get a letter from me?" cried God.

"Got one, yeah, but haven't read it yet," the ant prattled on, "been terribly busy," and he ran up God's left leg, above the knee. He was a red ant, and he took a bite.

"Stand still a minute, please, dear little ant," cried God, "I want to tell you something, or, if you prefer, ask you, about what you put in your cure-all wonder-oil, because mine. . . ." But when about ten thousand ants, all of them red, crawled up both his legs, he judged this wasn't the right moment for that chat he was so anxious to have for days now, even if it was with the least of his creatures. He shook them off.

Behind the woods the mountain slowly rose. He thought he heard something from back there. He walked in the direction of the falling darkness. Thursday evening.

In the twilight he saw someone sitting.

"How you, man?" he cried, thinking it might be an American black.

"I belong to a pop-group," the hare said, "and I'm just sitting here, listening."

"Is it beautiful?" cried God.

"Yes," the hare whispered. "Sh! there it is again."

They listened for several minutes.

"Beautiful!" cried God.

"It's a ram's horn," said the hare. "I really ought to go into the city to do a solo, but I'd rather listen to the ram's horn."

"Where is that ram's horn?" cried God.

"Sh!" said the hare, "I don't know. But it always comes from that direction, from behind the mountains."

"Always?" cried God.

"Yes, always, whenever I'm here."

"I'm going to go there. Will you come along?" cried God.

"No," said the hare, "I'm fine here; I can hear it."

"I'm off," said God, " 'bye, hare."

God walked till he reached the foot of the mountain. He heard "Yoo-hoo"—or something like that. He was tired. He sat down. Wild strawberries grew within reach of his hands, a stream spurted up from beneath a fallen tree.

"I like this spot," God thought, "I can hear it."

He dozed off. "Yoo-hoo" it wailed in his dream. He dreamt that he rose up, ran over the tops of the mountains as fast as flight, saw a stag with golden antlers. "Yoo-hoo." The sun tumbled over him like a laughing flower-girl, and the town was there, too, and he handed out pairs of flowers in abundance, and the chest with seven copper locks was still far from empty when he woke up. It grew dusk again. Friday evening.

"Sleeping away my precious time and still nothing accomplished," cried God.

Then he noticed that he was floating, lying on his back

in a kind of hatbox, or on something light as a feather—
a sleigh drawn by buffaloes and bears, flamingos and camels, all neatly spaced and in harness. And behind him
swayed the antique chest with the copper locks.

Elijah sat in the driver's seat, holding the reins.

"You were far away," he said.

"Yes," cried God, "yoo-hoo!"

"I just came down for a moment. Otherwise we may
never have seen you in heaven again, I fear. You still have
two days." "Two days!" cried God. "Then where are we
now?"

"Below us is the sea," said Elijah, "and in it, slowly and
imperceptibly, there moves an island, to and fro."

"I'm still dizzy from that dream," cried God. "What is
above us?"

"Above us, still other fiery earths zoom and roar, with
people just like us."

"Like us?" cried God.

"Today is Saturday," said Elijah. "Everybody on the
island is off today. They are all lying on the beach. Do
you think you can find your way by yourself now?"

"I guess I'll have to," cried God.

On the blond top of the dunes, the procession came to a
stop, with the flapping of wings and the growling of snouts.
God stepped out of the sleigh; he had become a naked
little child. He ran down the dunes. He saw a lady, reclin-
ing in a sand pit.

"Can you tell me how far it is, and how much it costs,
and how long it takes?" he cried.

The lady was sleeping. He walked to the next sand pit.
There two ladies were stretched out, done up in deep-sea
pearls. With them were some gentlemen, wearing painted
seaweed.

"Do you know how far it is, and how much it costs, and

how long it takes?" He wandered from one pit to another; glasses were taken off, eyes opened up.

Then, suddenly, he knew that he was in the wrong place. He ran to the edge of the sea, and beyond, out upon the surf, over the waves, naked. And the antique chest with seven locks, full of flowers tied in pairs, lay upon the open beach, at the edge of a sand pit. He ran on, leaping over one wave after the other.

Then he heard shouting from a distance. They had all climbed out of the sand pits, screaming, whistling, praying, and weeping, "We did not recognize Thee."

He gradually reduced his speed and came to rest. "Lord, Lord, it is Thou!" a woman's voice cried out, above the clamor. She had climbed up on the chest and was holding a telescope. "Thou, Lord!"

"Oh, no," God chuckled, "if all you people want me, you'll have to come after me. Leap upon the water, and it will bear you up; you'll easily overtake me, with so many. But you don't really want me."

In a matter of minutes, he had already disappeared from their sight.

Time for church. The bells rang, sad or joyous—people hustled along to praise him. He had an indefinable feeling. It was his last day, and there were not many creditable things he could report back home. He had a bite to eat at some snack bar, among the motorcycles, and in the late afternoon he began to ask the boys and girls, "Do you know where Abel Street is?"

"This way."

"No, that way."

He walked and walked. "Abel Street? That's on the other side of town."

Again the bells rang, and again people were on their way

to praise him. Suddenly he was in Abel Street. At Number 7 lived the chief rabbi. The heart of God leapt with joy. Elijah had planned his trip well, indeed.

But the closer he approached Number 7, the more nervous he became. "Just what is a chief rabbi?" God wondered. "Does he have wings like an archangel? Is he a kind of papa or pope, someone who knows a great deal about how things should be, and about me, too, and no doubt, someone who has only the best of intentions toward mankind? I wonder how he gets along with his children, and with the guilty and the innocent. Is he mild? Is he strong?"

But the chief rabbi was out. The sabbath had ended, his work-week had begun. "With all due respect to Elijah," he had thought, when he received the letter, "Elijah is not scripture." So he had gone out in the early evening, two thick scrolls under either arm, and in his head that passage from the prophet, "justice will I have, and not sacrifice." "A truth," thought the rabbi, "as big as a barn door, but how do you put it in everyday language?"

"Ah! Number 7," cried God. He rang. Nobody opened.

He grew sad. "I have such rotten luck," he cried, "I've been on the road a whole week now, to visit creatures, but I guess it's just not meant to be." He rang, waited. It began to rain. Sunday evening.

He rang once more. The doorway was quite narrow and he got wet. Rang again. Then he noticed that the rabbi lived in a twin house, and that the other half had an identical door and bell. He rang there, because he was soaking wet now.

A little boy opened the door and said, "My father is not at home." A man appeared.

"Are you not at home?" cried God.

"No," said the man, "but come in."

"I did not announce my coming," said God, "je m'excuse" (seeing a bust of Napoleon in the hall).

"What do you want?" said the man.

"Nothing, in fact," cried God.

"Don't cry out so hard," said the man, "I don't want anything either, but as long as you're here, who knows?"

Time passed quickly. They talked for hours. The little boy was long since in bed. They became friends.

"Do you want to be my son?" God suddenly asked. He was shocked by his own question, but he realized it was this very question which had driven him out of heaven on a whole week's journey.

"First of all," said the man, as he removed his glasses, "I am just as old as you are, I would judge. Secondly, are you quite sure you want to be my father?"

"What do you mean?" cried God.

"Can you wait up late at night for me? And can you do this: not curse me when I never have a word for you, and if I leave home and never return? And not always be crying out like that? Maybe I'll simply forget about you and simply feel relief when you die. Keep in mind, too, that I have a lot of brothers and sisters."

"I don't know," said God, "I really don't know and, actually, I must be going now. I'm a day late already."

"—and what about all those creatures," the man persisted, "who will crawl all over you, like ants, once they know you want to be their father? Can you put up with that, do you think?"

"Just ask Elijah," said God, mumbling his words for the first time in his life.

"Elijah didn't create us," said the man, "and he certainly didn't create the ants, either."

"I really have to be going now," said God, as he walked toward the door.

"Won't you be angry if we bear you no resemblance whatever?" asked the man. "Do you want to be our father for nothing?"

God was silent, his hand on the doorknob.

Then he said, "I want to try," and he began to weep. All the mountain streams and hidden wells broke loose in him.

"What am I doing, standing here weeping?" he said, after a while. "I must go, time is running out."

"You just go right ahead and weep," said the man, "who wouldn't weep at the sight of all those people?"

Then he added, "Yes, I want to be your son. See you later."

"See you," said God.

FOR THE DARKEST NIGHT OF THE YEAR

Me. four. six. nine. eighteen. thirty. thirty-eight
years. Where go, and how?

Fourteen. The tide had me in tow. Breakers wrapped
        me all
round, the mountainous water up over me then.

Then did you—lonely as you were,
lover lacking loved one, voice lacking echo,
man lacking friend—
then did you so persistently, burningly
knock at my door, I could not help but hear.
Then did you guide my feet and buttress my knees,
from every direction you spouted your life-giving breath,
gathered my bones, stretched over me
a new skin, a more sensitive membrane.
Then did you say to me: ghosts are a figment
but you exist,
then I became I, and you, whatever I think,
a God of people.

Now I have you in my head
like a whirlwind, a wild flood of notions.
Now like a bullseye, a shot in my heart
or a terrible hunch in my bones.
Full of your presence and full of your absence, I wait
all my life if I must
and I don't care who knows it.

For days I can think you away.
Like a new person. A burden lifted from me.
"Go to a land I shall show to you"—me?
rather mute than that I must answer
rather lame than that I must go.

My father knows me no more,
my mother backs me no more.
You have set me at odds with my fellows
and you have converted
my friends into strangers.

In the form of a dream you embraced me
last night. You were a tree
who wished to dance with me, then turned to fighting.
Fighting, you were changed to a dragon,
then to an angel, still later my son—
the hand
that stilled my weaponry, and tried and spared me.
Then I could enter into this new land.

Joy could not race as fast
as we would race, and lagged behind.
Sadness could not run as fast
as we would run, and lagged behind.
Grimly we stride forth,
the sky a graph of stacks and endless flames.

I wear the most expensive camouflage,
and spread myself across the thinnest words:
at times, yet, perhaps,
deny, don't see what I saw a moment before.
Dismiss, distinguish, or revoke
my former statement—such is life.
Yet you whom I have written
I have written.

Masks go off, other masks go on. Our party
numbered quite a few. And each of us did what he
    would.
An unforgettable evening.
But you,
as though the whole thing wasn't real
and you knew better,
you stood up straight, like a flute fluting on
in darkness, like marrow and honey and salt
in famine time.

Inventor of stars, firebrand
of the sun, and spark of the soul,
if I had you, if you were my friend
all would be well with me.

You are my stout crossbeam, thought I,
piling under my house, firm in my shifting sands,
my free-place, my nest high enough in the tree,
no beast reaches there.
I had no more need of hating.
I was given to see and be silent.

You came through closed-up doorways,
through a wall of Daily News.
You spoke through those famous words of old:

"I shall be there," and you were gone.
Along with all the dead
you went and died. Went where?

Surely you won't stone me
as a mother her child?
Surely you won't forget me
as a father his child?
You who, in the beginning, beat like a heart.

Lay my face bare, make me beautiful,
lay my face bare, make me beautiful—
I am impossibly rich.

Don't force my speaking. Cover my mouth.
Trap me. Win me. Elude me. Blind me.
Be subtle, inquiring, defiant.
Bashful. Affected. I dare you.

From one's suffocating emptiness
called and lifted out—can that be true?
I hope for feet and hands and shoulders,
eyes in a face brand-new and black.

To see you—that will be
like ivy flaming green out open windows
and no agenda. Breathing. Strolling in the sun,
no more dead-tired.
Shyly waiting. Learning stillness, fire,
the wheel, the shortest distance. Idly humming.
To see my friends again.

Dawning day. The early light
streaked over the meadow, over the bivouac,
over the bodies huddled and curled

lying asleep.
Then you came out of your tent, and you cried:
"It's turned to day, the light's appearing!
Why is it we do not rejoice?"

Notes

(All Notes are translators'. When two occur on same page, the second
Note is indicated below thus: **)

p. 1 Hadewych (13th-century Dutch mystic), *Visioenen.*

p. 5 For this line, the Dutch original reads merely *seen.* Revised by the
author for this translation.

p. 7 Hadewych, *Ritmata haiwigis* II, 21, lines 13, 14. Uitgegeven
door J. van Mierlo, Jr., S.J., Leuven, Keurboekerij, 1911.

p. 8 This poem, and those listed below, have been set to music, or
arranged, by the well-known Dutch composer, Bernard Huijbers:

     p. 21 (last 7 lines, titled) Even Then

     p. 43 Ye Gods

     p. 48 Winter Song

     p. 123 And Then

     p. 144 Song of the Sun

"Song at the Foot of the Mountain" is among the twenty-six
poems and psalm-translations of Oosterhuis, with music by
Bernard Huijbers, published under the title *Let My People
Sing: Songs and Biblical Hymns for Congregation and Choir,*
People's Edition, Book I, trans. by David Smith, Forrest Ingram,
Ger Groot and Redmond McGoldrick, North American Liturgy
Resources, 300 East McMillan Street, Cinn., Ohio 45219 (First
Printing, May 1974—"complete scores, choral editions, accompaniments and recordings are also available from the publisher.").
By arrangement with Seabury Press, New York.

  Additional Books in this series are in preparation—to include
the five poems listed above, and selections from other English
editions of Oosterhuis, notably *Fifty Psalms* (Oosterhuis, van
Beeck, van der Mas, Renkens, *et al,* Herder and Herder, New
York, 1969; paperback, Seabury Press, New York, 1974), with

textual revisions, and a few newly translated selections, by Redmond McGoldrick, in collaboration with Oosterhuis, Huijbers,
and Ger Groot.

p. 33 cf. Note to p. 8.

p. 29 heard on a TV interview with concentration camp survivors.

p. 30 Oosterhuis quotes an Old Dutch version of Isaiah 59:10. The
rhymed translation here is by Redmond McGoldrick.

p. 33 Lucebert (contemporary Dutch poet), *1948–1963 gedichten,*
De Bezige Bij, Amsterdam, 1965, p. 295, "Tijdtafel en Geslacht-
stabel." Oosterhuis quotes lines 6 and 8 again, p. 57, where line
7 has been inserted, and lines 10, 11 (in part), on p. 136.

p. 39 cf. preceding Note.

p. 41 Oosterhuis quotes these lines from *De goede mens van Sezuan,*
Gerrit Kouwenaar's Dutch translation (De Bezige Bij, Amsterdam, 1963, p. 67) of the original German, *De Gute Mensch von
Sezuan,* Bertolt Brecht, edition suhrkamp 73, 101–129. Tausend
1964. Copyright 1955 by Suhrkamp Verlag, Berlin, p. 62, lines
19–23. The English version used here is by Redmond McGoldrick.

p. 43 cf. Note to p. 8. Revision of an unpublished translation of
Forrest L. Ingram, with permission and grateful acknowledgment.

p. 48 cf. Note to p. 8.

p. 59 Luke 6:19: *indeed the whole crowd was trying to touch him
because power went out from him which cured all.* Luke 8:46:
*Jesus insisted, "Someone touched me; I know that power has
gone forth from me." The New American Bible* (hereafter:
NAB), Thomas Nelson, Inc., Camden, N.J., 1971. Copyright
Confraternity of Christian Doctrine, Washington, D.C., 1970. All
rights reserved. Unless otherwise noted, all bible quotations are
from this source.

Both general readers and, especially, students of theology,
who are well-versed in official Roman Catholic liturgical texts,
will no doubt be aware that those of Oosterhuis reflect a Chris-
tology different, at least in its emphases and orientation, from
that of the former. This is evident in the present essay, as in his
writings generally. For a brief scholarly treatment of this aspect
of the present book (and of his previous writings), see "Jezus of
Christus in het 'hooggebed,' " H. Manders, CSSR, *Tijdschrift
voor Theologie,* 13e Jaargang 1973, juli–aug.–sept., pp. 288–
309 (includes English Summary; also a parallel critique of
certain Eucharistic Prayers collected in *Eucharistic Liturgies:
Studies in American Pastoral Theology,* J. Gallen, S.J. [ed.],
New York, 1969).

p. 66 *NAB,* Proverbs 8:22, 24, 28a, 29a. The last verse quoted (31b) follows the Dutch bible, with Oosterhuis. *NAB* here reads: *and I found delight in the sons of men.*

p. 71 adaptations of *NAB*, Proverbs 8:22, 24, 28a.

p. 87 Dutch version, *NAB*, Acts 2:46, *in their homes.* ** e.g., Acts 22:4; 24:14, 22, in Lilly-Kleist and *RSV*. But *NAB: this (the) new way.*

p. 87 *NAB* I Corinthians 11:17–26. The Dutch of Oosterhuis is here a free but faithful rendition, with the exception indicated in the following Note.

p. 88 (I Corinthians 11:22) In *NAB, RSV,* and Lilly-Kleist, *intention* is rendered *church.*

p. 96 play on Dutch proverb: *He who does good meets good.*

p. 99 Revelations 2:17, as rendered by Oosterhuis from the Dutch version, which, however, reads *whoever conquers. NAB: to the victor.* Cf. Isaiah 62:26: *You shall be called by a new name/ pronounced by the mouth of the Lord.* Isaiah 65:15: *My servants shall be called by another name. (NAB)*

p. 100 *NAB*, Deuteronomy 30:19

p. 102 * Psalms 139:1, 2, 3b, 4, from *Viftig Psalmen*, Oosterhuis *et al.* (trans. by Redmond McGoldrick)
** Psalms 139: 13, 14, 15a. *Op. cit.* (trans. by Redmond McGoldrick)

p. 103 see pp. 78–81, *passim.*

p. 110 Guido Gezelle (19th century), *Kleengedichten.*

p. 111 Nescio, *Heimwee*, p. 8, Uits. G. A. van Oorchot, Amsterdam, 1962.

p. 115 The first two lines are from a Jewish "tabernacle song" by Clara Asscher-Pinkhof. The text is a song to the melody *Heer Halewijn song een liedekijn.*

p. 123 cf. Note to p. 8.

p. 131 Hendrik Marsman, *Verzameld Werk I*, "Heimwee," p. 55. Uitg. Querido, Amsterdam, 1947.

p. 136 Lucebert, *op cit.* (see Note to p. 33).

p. 138 paraphrase of Isaiah 52:15.

p. 139 *NAB*, Deut. 30:19 (a phrase is rearranged).

p. 142 Bertolt Brecht, *Gesammelte Werke*, "Die Tage der Commune," Suhrkamp Verlag, 1963.

p. 144 Revision of an unpublished translation of Forrest L. Ingram, with permission and grateful acknowledgment.